The Secret Club

By
Brianna Lindenmeyer

I hope this book is
an encouragement
and a reminder that
you are not alone!
With love,
[illegible]

Name: Brianna Lindenmeyer
Title: The Secret Club by Brianna Lindenmeyer
Identifiers: LCCN: Applied for
ISBN: 978-1-953114-32-7
Subjects: 1. Family and Relationships/Fertility and infertility
2. Health and Fitness/Pregnancy and Childbirth
3. Religion/Christian Living/Death, Grief, Bereavement

Unless otherwise noted, all Bible references *English Standard Version Bible*. Wheaton, Ill., Crossway Bibles, 2001

Published by EA Books Publishing, a division of

Living Parables of Central Florida, Inc. a 501c3

EABooksPublishing.com

Table of Contents

Prologue

1 in 8 couples struggle to conceive[1]

1 in 4 pregnancies end in a miscarriage[2]

1 in 5 women are childless, not by choice[3]

1 in 5 women struggle with secondary infertility[4]

Do you fall into one of these statistics? If your answer is yes, let me take a moment to welcome you to The Secret Club. This is the one of the few clubs where no one wants to be a member and nobody talks about it. However, as soon as you are in it, your eyes are opened to the hidden battles that are so consuming, yet kept silent—the battles of what is right or wrong or what to do next. The battle of continuously searching for solutions out of a desperation to fulfill a desire that is written on your heart. These battles awaken questions like why a perfect God made someone so broken, how can God give life and then just as quickly take it away, and "Why can I not have the desire that I long so deeply for?" The pain of even having to recognize your membership in this club can invoke feelings of loneliness, sadness, abandonment, and even embarrassment. This book is a window into the club for those who are not in it and a lifeline for those who are members, to remind you that you are not alone!

The Secret Club walks through my five-year journey of waiting and loss that I experienced from 2016 to 2021. Each chapter includes memories, painful moments, hard lessons, bad decisions, and delicate emotions. Along with my story, between each chapter you will find seven other women's stories. Each of these women is a member of the secret club in their own unique way.

Beyond the stories and testimonies, the backbone of this book includes passages of scriptures from *The Holy Bible* that have been woven into my story. Each verse, story, or passage has guided and encouraged me through every step forward or backwards in my journey. My words could never offer you the grace and encouragement that is offered by the Word of God.

You may ask, "Well why the Bible? Why do I need to read scriptures?"

Since my sophomore year in college, Jesus Christ has been the cornerstone in my life, and despite the hardships I face, He does not abandon me. Through reading the Bible, I am opening my ears to hear God speak to me, guide me, love me, and remind me that I am not alone. He speaks to my weary soul and gives me strength, hope, and a future. He protects me from the weight of the world, and with each word from the Bible that you read in this book, he will speak to you too. As you see passages in this book, do not skim through them or skip ahead; instead, pause, read, re-read, highlight, circle verses that stand out to you. This process allows God to use His word to speak absolute truth into your life.

At the beginning of each chapter, you will see a segment from Psalms 31. The book of Psalms was written by David and a few other authors. Each psalm is intended as a poem or song and was the author's outlet for communicating with the Lord through everyday struggles and deep valleys. Together, all 150 psalms show a beautiful and complete picture of the emotions of the heart.

About a one-and-a-half years into my journey with infertility, I was drawn to the book of Psalms. Each morning, I read a psalm and this taught me how to cry out to God, how to ask from God while honoring His will. These scriptures showed me so much about the love God had for David and also how much God loved all of His people, including me.

As days, months and years passed, I experienced waiting, pregnancy, loss, and more waiting. but despite the event, it seemed as though each day I was given the exact psalm and encouragement that I needed. I encountered emotions I did not know were even possible, along with experiences of loss, loneliness, and even confusion on what I was supposed to be doing. As I looked back through my Bible after our miscarriage, I saw three words I had written these words next to Psalm 31, *"Found out pregnant."* I reread that and noticed that this particular psalm reflected years of the experience that I had. This Psalm talked about the loneliness, grief, waiting and most importantly, Psalm 31 showed me the hope that I was searching for with every step I took. I felt so comforted by the thought that God would have chosen to give me Psalm 31 on the exact day that I found out I was pregnant with our child. Not only would this scripture bring me comfort, but it would also be the road map of our journey.

Digging into this psalm brought me refuge in my time of heartbreak. The verses in Psalm 31 led me to see the divine plan the Lord had for my life. This psalm guided my writing of this book, along with other scriptures, stories, and hard lessons I learned with each step I took.

Many women walk the journey of infertility, infant, or pregnancy loss, but the path feels lonely, isolating, and difficult. It can leave you feeling as though you are the only one struggling and trying to fight for this desire to have a child. As we mentioned earlier, other members of this secret club have graciously written out their stories for you throughout this book to share, encourage you, and give you something to relate to. You are not alone, and I hope that by the end of this book, you see that and are open to how God is using this very journey to be a testimony of His love and power.

I want to encourage you to read through Psalm 31 and

highlight or make note of any verse that stands out to you. Write as much or as little as you would like.

Psalm 31

In you, O Lord, do I take refuge; let me never be put to shame; in your righteousness deliver me! Incline your ear to me; rescue me speedily! Be a rock of refuge for me, a strong fortress to save me!

For you are my rock and my fortress; and for your name's sake you lead me and guide me; you take me out of the net they have hidden for me, for you are my refuge. Into your hand I commit my spirit; you have redeemed me, O Lord, faithful God.

I hate those who pay regard to worthless idols, but I trust in the Lord. I will rejoice and be glad in your steadfast love, because you have seen my affliction; you have known the distress of my soul, and you have not delivered me into the hand of the enemy; you have set my feet in a broad place.

Be gracious to me, O Lord, for I am in distress; my eye is wasted from grief; my soul and my body also. For my life is spent with sorrow, and my years with sighing; my strength fails because of my iniquity, and my bones waste away.

Because of all my adversaries I have become a reproach, especially to my neighbors, and an object of dread to my acquaintances; those who see me in the street flee from me. I have been forgotten like one who is dead; I have become like a broken vessel. For I hear the whispering of many—terror on every side! —as they scheme together against me, as they plot to take my life.

But I trust in you, O Lord; I say, "You are my God." My times are in your hand; rescue me from the hand of my enemies and from my persecutors! Make your face shine on your servant; save me in your steadfast love! O Lord, let me not be put to shame, for I call upon you; let the wicked be put to shame; let them go silently to

Sheol. Let the lying lips be mute, which speak insolently against the righteous in pride and contempt.

Oh, how abundant is your goodness, which you have stored up for those who fear you and worked for those who take refuge in you, in the sight of the children of mankind! In the cover of your presence you hide them from the plots of men; you store them in your shelter from the strife of tongues.

Blessed be the Lord, for he has wondrously shown his steadfast love to me when I was in a besieged city. I had said in my alarm, "I am cut off from your sight." But you heard the voice of my pleas for mercy when I cried to you for help.

Love the Lord, all you his saints! The Lord preserves the faithful but abundantly repays the one who acts in pride. Be strong, and let your heart take courage, all you who wait for the Lord!

Chapter 1 - Running the Race

In you, O Lord, do I take refuge; let me never be put to shame; in your righteousness deliver me! Incline your ear to me; rescue me speedily! Be a rock of refuge for me, a strong fortress to save me! — Psalm 31:1–2

I was never much of a student. I did not look forward to school, but on this day of my junior year, I was excited to go to classes. I got up early, had my mom do my hair in two French braids, not one, put on a cross-country shirt, and went to school. I was taking a class called Child Growth and Development. In this class we studied children and their motor skills milestones, created lessons for preschool students, took care of an infant doll, and even watched a live birth, which made me close my eyes. My mind was not ready to view all *that* quite yet.

On this day, we would get to walk around during class wearing a pregnancy prosthesis—third-trimester belly and breasts—to experience the weight and feeling of being pregnant. We all took turns, and I remember getting to finally walk around the school wearing the belly. I was so excited. As I walked down the hall with my idea of cute, pregnant-woman hair and my waddle that was forced due to a massive belly on my little high school body, I placed my hand under this belly and thought about one day having a miracle of life growing inside of me.

Pure joy filled me as I thought about the time in my life when

I would be able to be pregnant. I was not in a rush, I was only in high school, but I still remember that day, and the deep breath of excitement that I felt at the thought of one day being pregnant.

To this day, I sometimes flash back to that feeling in the school hallway. I feel this umbrella of foreshadowing that covers that innocent high school moment. What if I could go back and tell myself as a young girl with two French braids that my dream of one day being pregnant and starting a family would be the hardest, longest, most lonely journey that I would face? Would I still want it? Would I still fight for it? Would I have made the same choices? Why would God give me this moment that I have held onto for all these years and not allow me the full and real thing?

As of July 2020, 7,794,798, 739 people were on this planet. The population continues to increase by about 1 percent each year. Watching the population clock increase and decrease more quickly than I can register what the number is makes me realize just how small my life is. A number—I am one of those 7.8 billion. Of those 7.8 billion people in the world, 49.6 percent are females. I am one of those 3,866,220,174 females. In the United States, of the 160.22 million females, approximately 75 million are within ages 15 to 50 years. One in eight of those women have had, will have, or are currently having trouble conceiving. About 900,000 females in the United States battle the question of how to create a new life, and face the frustrations of seeking information, help, treatment, and interventions.

I am one of those 900,000 females in a quiet, lonely, secret club that some do not realize exists but is all others can think about. Ninety percent of women struggling to conceive can receive medical treatment or intervention to help them conceive. Ten percent of couples struggling with infertility have unknown reasons for infertility and are left with no answer. I am one of those 900,000 with no answers from this world.

As I read through these numbers, I can feel my mind build walls around me. It isolates me into this category of people. This group of 1 in 8, these 900,000 women who, despite their wants, desires, cries, and prayers, cannot have a child at the timing they want. Questions fill my mind of "Why? Why me? At age twenty-four am I damaged goods?" A mistake must have occurred when I was made because I want to be a mother so much, but my body is not working. The walls close in around me; I feel the loneliness and the weight of being that one in eight.

Sometimes it is hard to awaken from these numbers. The numbers themselves are not a lie, but the dark funnel my mind puts me in as I read and isolate myself is a lie. I face the feeling and discouragement of settling into the idea that I am just one of those numbers. One of those eight women who will never have answers and will never be able to live out my true purpose of being a mother.

That is a lie from Satan. To Jesus Christ, I am not a number. I have a purpose that is greater than any number that describes my circumstances. God sees numbers in a different way. He knows the number of hairs on my head (Luke 12:7). He knows every upset, every tear, every heartbreak, and every hurt (Psalm 56:8). He chose me (John 15:16). He designed me (Psalm 139:14). And He will never forsake me (Joshua 1:9). And the situation, circumstance, or the question I am lost in is not a mistake. God has designed a course for my life, and He does not make mistakes.

From a young age, running has been my sport and my outlet. I found a love for cross country, not track. I was terrible at track. I tried to run track one year but was assigned to long distance because of my success as a cross-country runner. However, I could not handle the eight times I had to run on the same circle. During a race I would literally go on autopilot and just countdown the seconds till the race was over. Honestly, I could finish at the back of the pack and would regret not trying harder or pushing myself more.

Running long distance track was similar to how my life was before I began following Jesus Christ. It was repetitive, and I tried to stay in the middle of the pack for as long as possible. I saw the routine and pattern of the American dream and wanted that series of events to happen as I expected in my life. After you had run one lap, you now had an expectation set for you by everyone watching, because they knew your ability. In running track, one race is the same race as all the others. Around and around the same circle, just with different people. Same result.

Cross country was different for me; I loved the changes and challenges around every turn on a course. There is a sense of adrenaline, new competition, and a new focus. I felt the energy surge in me as I powered up a hill, rounded a corner, or dug in deep for the sprint to the finish uphill 400 meters. When I crossed that finish line, I felt my body had given everything it had; I could not even think about moving or drinking water; I just wanted to see my family and friends, to relive the last eighteen minutes of my life.

The minute I started following Christ, the gun went off, and my race began. The first 100 meters after the start of a cross-country race is a sprint; people are fired up, they are running on a surge of adrenaline to get in their placement for the race.

Starting your relationship with Christ follows a familiar pattern—you start off being on fire for Christ and wanting to spread the good news to the world. After about 100 meters, your placement starts to settle and so does your pace. You start to fall back to a comfortable race pace, while going through hills, valleys, rocks, and mud. Once you know you are in the last mile, you pick it up and give all you have to get through every obstacle fighting every inch to reach that finish line.

Becoming a follower of Jesus Christ changes the focus of your life. God created the heavens and the Earth, every plant, animal, man and woman with the purpose of glorifying Him in a perfect world but sin came into existence and separated God and humans. People could not live eternally with God, so God sacrificed His only Son, who took on the wrath of God and paid the price so we can live eternally with Him. If you are a follower of Christ, you believe you are a sinner and need to repent of your sins. You understand that apart from Jesus, you would live eternally in hell for your sin. You would live in a place that does not have God, because God cannot be with sin. Jesus paid the ultimate price of death as a perfect man so that he can cover our sins in the presence of God. When you believe and commit yourself to Jesus Christ, you get a new spirit.

In eternity we will get a new body but for now, we have a new spirit in a worldly, fleshly body. God sends a gift to his followers—the Holy Spirit. The Holy Spirit lives within you and guides your new spirit. The Holy Spirit will give you guidance and grow your spirit to be like Christ, if you choose to listen to Him.

Every course designed for a cross-country race is different and unique. They all have elements that can be challenging or difficult to different runners. The course for my life is, likewise, different than anyone else's. It was designed specifically for me. God designed it for me, and he is a perfect God who does not make mistakes. At times my course crosses paths with people who share some of the same obstacles but the journey that led us there and the course could look different. In a race, I would seek the portions of the course that would give me great difficulty, and I would ask my family, friends, or coaches to be in specific areas of the course. Hearing my name screamed and words of encouragement as I struggled through obstacles and fought the mental battle of taking one more step.

Life does not get easier after you put your faith in Christ as your Savior. In fact, you will probably notice it getting more difficult. Your eyes have been opened to the spiritual battles that occur every day and the obstacles for the course you are on. You have been taken off the track and put on a course designed for you. Your course will have hills and valleys, and you will have no idea how to cross—but with the guidance of the Holy Spirit, you will.

The reward of spending eternity with Christ is wondrous, and this life is meant to develop your spirit to be ready for your new body in eternity. This battle is priceless and worth the fight. Throughout the battle, you will feel the pressures and pains from this world, but you will also see Christ in a way that you could never imagine. You will see Christ show up, and you will feel His presence in the darkest of times, recognize His miracles are ever present, identify the impression that He leaves on people every day, and experience the greatest peace in knowing you have a heavenly father who is always there for you and will never leave your side.

When you live without Christ, you seek and experiment to try to fill that hole of loneliness that we have without Christ. Jesus Christ has a plan for you. He has set a course for your life, and at the finish line, He will be waiting to hold you and not let go.

The race has started, the gun has fired, you are in a full sprint to start the course that Christ has you on. It feels pretty easy for a minute, but then your course leads you into your first obstacle. Throughout our lives as Jesus followers, we run into trials and temptations. As you read through the Bible, you will hear these words and they will seem synonyms.

They tend to run together when people are talking about hardships, but it is important to distinguish the two.

Trials are obstacles that God puts on our course for us to overcome with His power and wisdom. Trials can be hardships, challenges, things that happen to us, deaths, births, and changes. God uses trials to mold your new spirit into who He wants you to be and, ultimately, to bring Him glory.

My trial is trying to conceive a child. My trial started back in 2016. We were ready, we had a home, a church, family close by, our age was right, our bodies were good, our income was sufficient, and we were ready. When we started, we did not think this would be a trial for us due to neither of our parents having difficulties conceiving. As we took our first steps onto this obstacle, we had no idea that we were on a gradual incline leading to a large mountain. We were clueless. After a few months of trying for a child, we started to feel winded, and we started questioning what was going on. Months led to a year, and still we had empty arms, an empty womb and, at moments, empty hope.

This hardship has molded me. I have had good moments and weak moments, but it is an opportunity to bring glory to God, even in the painful, unfair moments (more about that later). These obstacles, hills, or trials are meant to grow our new spirit, so we must rely on God to shave off and sharpen the parts of us that are weak.

My weakness was my desire for a child. So many times I wished for a different trial or a different obstacle to overcome. *God, can you pick another area to grow my spirit? This one seems too hard, too painful, and too lonely.* I wanted a child so bad; I was willing to give God whatever other area He wanted, but not this one. As followers of Christ, trials are obstacles that we should expect. They are a sharp way that we stand out in a culture. When we handle a common disappointment by pointing to Christ, we show our reliance and trust in God when all else seems to fail. We show that our focus is on our eternity with Christ and not on the boundaries of this life.

All throughout my trial of infertility, I had this constant desire to have a child. The desire itself is not bad. God gave me the desire to one day have children. However, at times my desire to have children took my eyes off the end goal of serving Christ and put it on my immediate desire. I would focus on finding a shortcut to get around the obstacle instead of staying on the course and enduring the hill; that was the temptation.

Now remember the new spirit we are given when we follow the Lord? Well, the new spirit is trapped in an old, sinful, fleshy body that is of this world. That sinful, fleshy body is drawn to doing works of the evil one, Satan. The goal of Satan is to draw us away from God. Satan does this by using human feelings of anger, jealousy, lust, and hatred to pull our focus on our fleshly body, on the here and now, not the forever.

Satan creates shortcuts that appear to be good and feel good to our fleshly bodies, but lead us to an empty place or a dead end. Satan's goal is to pull our eyes to focus on the emotions, the desires, and the pleasures that seem satisfying, but leave you empty and vulnerable for destruction. If I am seeking a shortcut while running, I cannot also be following the course. These temptations are meant to distract from the obstacle God has given to mold you to be like Him.

Shortcuts were revealed when I let jealousy rule my eyes and lust fill my heart. I was tempted to not take another step on the obstacle designed for me and instead seek solutions that I could plan and control. Temptations are the voices of this world and inside yourself that distract you from God. When you give in to the temptations, you are not following

Christ; you are following the ways of the evil one whose path only leads to destruction.

As I started up this gradual incline of a trial, Kyle and I would pray for a child. Every time someone asked for a prayer request, we were ready to share our desire for a child. *Lord, give us a child.* God gave the command to *"Be fruitful and multiply." (Genesis 1:28)* to Adam and Eve after the creation and then to Noah and his family after the flood. God is all for reproduction. We are two God-loving people, God gave us the desire; this should be a "cake walk."

As we started up this trial, a hesitation hung out in the back of my mind that wondered, "What if this does not happen and God does not answer my prayers?"

I was not ready to come to grips with that idea so I hid it and continued to look for successes in the Bible and scripture to pray to the Lord. One common way people in my situation would manipulate the Bible was pointing to James 4:2 and saying the scripture says, "Ask and you shall receive." I was asking, but I was not receiving. I was hoping, but the Lord was not showing up in the way that I wanted Him to.

As much as I wished for the statement in James to be my outcome, it was not. God is a loving, all-knowing, all-powerful, and sovereign Father. This verse does not say to ask for anything you want and God will automatically give it to you, it actually starts the phrase in verse 5: *"If any of you lacks wisdom, let him ask God, who gives generously to all without reproach, and it will be given him" (James 1:5).*

The confusing part of James 1:5 and the reason it is commonly manipulated is in reference to the portion about asking. God promises us if we ask for wisdom, He will always give us the insight or the step we need to get through a trial—He won't necessarily give us what we want. He will give us a path on our course to overcome the trial.

It took a year to get off the emotional roller coaster of self-pity and discouragement to start trying to figure out how *God* wanted me to get through this trial, instead of determining how *I* wanted to get through this trial. I asked for wisdom about the step that He wanted me to take, and He answered. He answered through His Word, the Bible. During the following weeks, God's answer to me was confirmed through people, music, and things that happened. He answered. He gave me the way through.

You may be asking, what did He say? What was your answer? I want you to remember that God answers the same trials differently for each person. Our obstacles may be similar, but our courses leading to and following are different. My answer is not your answer. Sometimes He says yes or no and shows you your next steps, and sometimes He says wait. My answer was wait. Not "Wait and try this." Just wait.

Maybe you are saying, "That's it? That was His answer? That did not solve anything. You still do not have a child."

But that gave me peace beyond understanding. The God who created the universe, who breathes life into creation, said,

"I have not forgotten about you, just wait, My timing is perfect. My times are in your hands; deliver me from the hands of my enemies, from those who pursue me. Let your face shine on your servant; save me in your unfailing love. Let me not be put to shame, Lord, for I have cried out to you." — Psalm 31:15–17

The urgency to try a bunch of solutions or keep trying to scheme my way into getting pregnant was taken off the table. God wanted me to wait, and wait is what I was going to do.

Waiting was hard. It was hard to see new babies, scroll to someone's pregnancy announcement on Facebook, and type the words, "So happy for you!" as tears streamed down my face. It was difficult to watch moms holding, breastfeeding, loving and nurturing their little ones. I would feel that overwhelming yearning come upon me. A sense of urgency would hit me, like my time was running out, and I would endure and remember God's answer to me: *Just wait, my timing is perfect, just wait.*

Not wavering was hard. I wish I could say I was always successful at fighting off temptations, but I was not. Many times, someone would ask me when we were going to have children, and I would say what God had told me. They would respond with advice on how they or friends were able to get pregnant. It took everything inside of me to just say, "I am really glad that (blank) worked for them. Isn't it great how God answers us? I feel like God is asking me to just wait right now so I want to be obedient."

They would be thrown off from my lack of interest in a solution. I did not know what to say and neither did they, so their way of encouragement was offering a way to fix my "problem." They would try to give me a sense of hope, but the truth is, those solutions are not hope if they are not aligned with God's plan. They are distractions, temptations, and ways to take our focus off of what God wants us to do. They pull our attention from the trial at hand.

But let him ask in faith, with no doubting, for the one who doubts is like a wave of the sea that is driven and tossed by the wind. —James 1:6

After James said to ask for wisdom of how to get through the trial and it will be given, He adds a warning. This warning was so relevant in my journey: Ask in faith, but do not doubt. Again, he was not talking about asking in faith that we would be given something but instead, asking for the wisdom to get through the trial and not doubt His answer. You'd better bet that if God gives us the way through our trial, our temptations from the evil one will try to get us to doubt the instructions God gave us.

Stephen Armstrong, pastor of Verse-by-Verse Ministries International, has told this story:

A father had a teenage son who was involved in vandalizing a public park.

The father was unsure what to do; this crime would affect his son's ability to get a job and affect his future. He asked God what to do as a father. God gave him wisdom and understanding to let the son reap the full consequence from the law. The court date was coming up and he felt at peace with his decision in letting his son take the sentence.

The day before his court date, a guy at his work told him about a way that he could pay off the judge, and the judge would release him with a warning. The father was so excited because this seemed like an answer to prayer and a solution that was even better for his son.

So, the father went back to the Lord in prayer and asked about this new solution to the problem. Should he take it? He did not hear anything from the Lord. The Lord was silent. The father went ahead and took the deal because it seemed like the way out, and he paid off the judge.

The son was released with a warning and went on to commit larger crimes and wound up back in prison serving sentences that put strife on the family.

Why was God silent? Why did He not say, "No, do not take the deal"?

God gave His answer at the start, and that was the step the father was instructed to take. It was the wisdom that he asked for. The father then wavered, found another solution, and took the advice from a man who was not the all-knowing, all-powerful and sovereign God.

God does not answer people who waver like the ocean. I cannot tell you how many that I have done this. I would seek other solutions, then feel distant from God and wonder why He was not answering me. I am not saying that God does not use people to give us guidance, but it will align with what He is telling you through His Word and through His spirit.

How do I know if I am wavering? How do I know whether what I hear is actually the Lord or if it is just the voice in my head? God uses people, advertisements, doctors, signs, events, etc. but those same things are also used by the evil one to distract us and lead us off the course that has been designed for us. They are temptations and take us away from completing the trial we are on. Any answer from the Lord will align with the Bible.

A way to check is to ask the Lord, and then read the scriptures and listen, instead of seeking for the answers that you would like to hear from Him. Just listen and be patient. He will answer you as you read and as you wait. It is really easy to talk over His answer, but fight the urge and allow the Holy Spirit to show you through scripture what to do.

Sometimes if I do not hear from Him right away, I worry that I have missed something or did not hear the answer, but the truth is, if you are seeking Him and reading His word, He will not let you miss His plan.

How do I know if I heard Him correctly? If I am doing what the Lord wants, I have God on my side. He will encourage me through His words, acts, and His people. He is going to help and guide me. I have a sense of assurance and hope because God is on my side.

If the solution is from my desires or feelings, God will not encourage me to take this path. This will result in a sense of distance between God and me, and I will seek someone to be on my side.

As humans, we do not like to be alone. You can see this in our culture. People living in sin look for others to agree with them that they are doing the right thing and have a sense of belonging and empowerment. We seek justification that we are in the right and doing good works. In my infertility, I knew God wanted me to wait, but I would seek and research solutions that could "fix my problem."

A sense of guilt surrounded me when I would find an option that seemed like a good fit. Instead of taking that guilt to the Lord, I would seek people who would side with me and tell me that this solution was the right choice for me. I felt as though I could do this all on my own, but the minute I left those people and was alone, I felt that same empty feeling. It was the feeling of disobedience. I was feeling the distance that sin puts between my Father and me.

However, despite my seeking other answers, God stayed consistent. He waited for me with arms wide open—just patiently waiting for me to turn my eyes and focus back on Him.

During my years of running cross country, I had a coach who stood out from the others—Tim Nixon. He was an amazing coach. He took an interest in every one of his runners. He challenged us, encouraged us and told very long, drawn-out stories that I heard fifty times. Those stories were inspirational and encouraged us to endure practices, races, successes, and failures.

I had the privilege to run alongside his daughter. She was one of the top racers for the team, but like all runners, she had great races and she had ones that she looked back on and wished she could have done better. I remember her running half of one race with only one shoe on because it had gotten stuck in mud. But she persevered. She continued to run and did not stop to give a second thought. What a gal!

At Tim Nixon's funeral, his daughter spoke about how sometimes when she ran, she expected a lecture or was embarrassed by her performance. However, every time, good or bad, he took her in his arms and told her how proud he was of her.

What a beautiful picture of what our heavenly father does for us. As we run this race that is full of trials, hardships, temptations, He gives us guidance through His word and the Holy Spirit and is waiting for us at our finish line. He stands at the finish line with arms open wide to catch us, hold us, and never let go. So why do we endure these trials? Why do we choose God's ways instead of shortcuts or search for satisfaction in the world? I do this because when I cross that finish line and God embraces me, I want Him to say:

Well done, good and faithful servant! You have been faithful with a few things; I will put you in charge of many things. Come and share your master's happiness!" —Matthew 25:21

Questions for Reflection:

If you had to draw out a course for your life up till now, what obstacles would you say have been in your way?

____

____

How did you overcome them?

____

____

What or who was your biggest motivator?

____

____

What trial are you facing right now?

____

____

In what ways is Satan trying to get you to waver on your course?

____

____

Are you distracted by any shortcuts?

____

____

What is your reason for finishing the race strong?

____

____

Secret Club Member: Morgan Pfaff

My Story:

Chad and I got married later in life, so everyone we knew was already having kids or in the process of being a parent. I felt very alone as we started trying for children.

At about 10 months into the process, my OB offered a referral and also offered to prescribe me Clomid. I was slightly taken back by how quickly this process was moving. *Should we run tests and see why we are not successful? Maybe there is a reason that I am not getting pregnant,* I thought.

Time ticked on, and we progressed in our testing and also in our findings. We found out that we had both female and male infertility factors, and our chances of a successful pregnancy were limited naturally. Our chances of IVF were only 5 percent, so we proceeded with IUI treatments. Intrauterine Insemination (IUI) is a procedure in which the sperm specimen is washed and concentrated and placed directly in the uterus at the time of ovulation.

We felt the weight of the constant comments of "When are you going to have kids?" "Do you want me to show you how to get the job done?" Or "Just get drunk."

Our response was, "Do you really think we haven't tried?"

My bitterness grew towards people, and I only hung out with my tribe, who told me supportive things or just held my hand and said, "This sucks." They loved me and knew my story. No one knows what you are going through unless they have gone through it themselves.

At this point, we had completed five IUI treatments and were completing our sixth round when I got the positive pregnancy result. We told the family and bought a fun onesie. It was super early, but this was what we had been praying for, and we wanted the support and prayers from our family. This was such an exciting time! Not to mention that my sister-in-law was also pregnant with a baby due two weeks before ours. We were thrilled that these two cousins would grow up together.

I was monitored regularly with IUI treatments, but my numbers were not elevating as they should have been. The doctor came to the conclusion that the baby was stuck in my fallopian tubes, so I was instructed to go home and come back the next day, when they would give me a shot. They told me my body would then push out the embryo. If I felt any pain, I was to go to the ER because my tubes could explode and make me bleed out.

I ended up with intense pain. We went to the ER, and I received several shots. The ER ultrasound tech found our baby, so I was grateful we could actually see it. They sent me home and I passed our baby. I felt so alone. I distanced myself from family and friends to reduce the risk of harsh comments and tension.

We met with a new specialist. We discussed the fact that IUIs simply were not working. We decided to proceed with the next step in fertility treatment: IVF. As we walked to the truck to drive around to the front of the hospital to make a $5000.00 deposit for the IVF treatment, I heard God tell me that we needed to adopt. I felt an instant weight lifted and I told Chad what I had just felt God tell me.

He said, "let's do it!"

So we left without paying a penny towards IVF, and we were so excited to start exploring the option of adoption. This was the first time we had ever *both* felt a sense of relief and clarity.

Looking back, I did not realize that I was that far in the trenches until I was on the other side—the darkness and loneliness, the feeling of being uneasy and uncertain in the steps we were taking and the boxes we were checking off. We prayed countless prayers throughout this storm, but at the beginning, our prayers were pleading for a baby. After our ectopic pregnancy, we started questioning, "Why are we doing this? Lord, what do you want for us because we know you have given us the desires to be parents, but what route do you want us to take? Show us the path".

When my prayers changed from what we were requesting to being open to what the Lord wanted for us, His path for us was made crystal clear.

When we took the step of adoption, I felt joy and ease as we started walking down the route that the Lord wanted. We both felt a weight being lifted off our shoulders. We applied through an open adoption facility and in 11 months, we were holding our sweet baby girl, Mason. We held her on her first day of life. She was 8 pounds, 7 ounces, and 19 inches long. Her first mama was so supportive of Chad and me, that she felt as though Mason was designed to be our daughter.

Before we walked into that room to meet our daughter, we faced questions about adoption, such as: What would that be like? Would we bond? Would she feel like mine?

But the minute I held her, she was our precious baby girl! We were finally parents.

Did a scripture or song stick with you during your journey?

Anything on KLOVE—it would always encourage me and move my focus onto the Lord. "Who You Say I Am" by Hillsong Worship was special, as well as the scripture that says, "Love Never Fails," (1 Corinthians 13:8). God was hearing me, and the desires from my heart. His love alone would satisfy all my desires.

What is something that always makes you remember your journey?

Fertility and miscarriage awareness months always remind me of our journey.

What would you say to a woman who is going through something similar?

I love you! Keep going! You are a mom; you were meant to be a mom! Pray. No fixing things; just keep taking one step at a time because it is so long and so hard.

Chapter 2 - Prepare for Battle

For you are my rock and my fortress; and for your name's sake you lead me and guide me; you take me out of the net they have hidden for me, for you are my refuge. Into your hand I commit my spirit; you have redeemed me, O Lord, faithful God. —Psalm 31:3–5

Waiting to get pregnant, felt like forever. Each month, I started out so strong-willed and hopeful that this month would be the one when the nine-month countdown would begin.

I started the month being the healthiest I could be, I would run, eat well, and spend lots of intimate time with my husband. Around my ovulation time, I would get excited, but I would remind myself of the feelings of previous months and tell myself I would not get worked up about it. I was just going to do my best to trust that the Lord was going to come through, and if it happened . . . great.

Another week went by and I would look for any sign of pregnancy. Fatigue . . . maybe it's a sign. My nipples hurt if I pinch them . . . maybe it's a sign.

I cannot tell you how many times I googled, "SUPER early signs of pregnancy" or "Is (blank) a sign of pregnancy?" I could always find someone (medical website, blogger, chat sites, etc.) who had recorded whatever feeling I was going through as a symptom of early pregnancy.

That last week was the worst as I counted down the days till I could take a pregnancy test. Sometimes I would sneak a test early, but when only one line would show up, I would then convince myself it was too early—many other women had gotten false pregnancy tests, and then days later it would be positive due to HCG levels (thanks Google!).

Many times, I would start to feel intense feelings, slight cramps, sensitive breasts, fatigue, or slightly nauseated. I tended to look up the due date calculator so that I could imagine and dream of what the birth and newborn stage would be like in the month the child would be born. I would convince myself to wait just one more day.

I would wake up, do my normal routine, read scripture, pray and journal that if I were pregnant, that the Lord would show it to me so that I could stop waiting. I would then continue with my day. Typically, that same day, I would feel a slight twinge, and then all my symptoms would simply go away. I would pray for it to not be true and decided maybe if I just avoid checking, then maybe I could hold onto the fantasy just a little longer.

At a time when my hormones were so high, it was hard to go to the restroom and come to grips with the unwelcomed monthly visitor. I would shed tears and sometimes silently cry out in a public area. Then I would splash cold water on my face and return to the work with no one wiser of my inner turmoil.

In those moments, what could I say? "I am upset that my period came, and I wanted a baby. I am upset because my heart desires a child, and it will not happen. I am upset because I am embarrassed that I wasted time obsessing over this day that I knew would probably come. I am upset that I am going to have to tell my husband. I am upset I spent all that money on wasted pregnancy tests. I am upset because the girl across the room from me just got pregnant with her third child. I am upset that I have to wait."

I was in a trap of broken expectations and disappointments. I would convince myself that I was just unlucky to be among the

1 in 8 who would struggle with getting pregnant. Someone had to be the one, so, of course, it had to be me, someone who wanted a child so badly.

These thoughts would funnel me into a dark place where I felt alone and silenced. I was stuck in a trap—not a trap made by this world, but a trap for my mind and spirit. Satan had set a trap along my trial, and I had fallen right in.

Satan is tricky; he will use things like normalcy, emotions, and doubt. I was so focused on the end step of holding a baby in my arms that my focus was not on where my next step was meant to be, or better yet, what the Lord was really trying to do with the situation.

The truth sets you free from hidden traps laid by Satan. No matter what the circumstances—whether you are drowning in your emotions, lost in doubt, or alone in darkness—God will find you and rescue you if you search for Him.

Where can I go from your Spirit? Where can I flee from your presence? If I go up to the heavens, you are there; if I make my bed in the depths, you are there. If I rise on the wings of the dawn, if I settle on the far side of the sea, even there your hand will guide me, your right hand will hold me fast. If I say, "Surely the darkness will hide me and the light become night around me," even the darkness will not be dark to you; the night will shine like the day, for darkness is as light to you. —Psalm 139:7–12

These long months continued and turned into a year of trying. I started to question, *Is "wait" still my answer from God? Has he forgotten about me? What the heck are we waiting on?*

Questioning is a part of human nature, and we question things we do not understand.

I am going to take you back a long time ago—and I mean a

long, long time ago—to a paradise: *"In the beginning..."*

Eve, the perfect woman. She was the perfect wife with the best husband and wife relationship—no trust issues, comparing, shame, or guilt of her past. She had a perfect relationship with the Lord and walked side-by-side with Him. She lived in a literal garden where she worked joyously and was even a vegetarian. Eve had it all.

God gave Adam and Eve one direct instruction about life in the garden:

"And the Lord God commanded the man, "You are free to eat from any tree in the garden; 17 but you must not eat from the tree of the knowledge of good and evil, for when you eat from it you will certainly die" (Genesis 2:16–17).

No one knows how long Adam and Eve lived in this paradise before things took a turn for the worse because they could not follow that one simple rule:

Now the serpent was more crafty than any of the wild animals the Lord God had made. He said to the woman, "Did God really say, 'You must not eat from any tree in the garden'?"

The woman said to the serpent, "We may eat fruit from the trees in the garden, but God did say, 'You must not eat fruit from the tree that is in the middle of the garden, and you must not touch it, or you will die.'"

"You will not certainly die," the serpent said to the woman. "For God knows that when you eat from it your eyes will be opened, and you will be like God, knowing good and evil."

When the woman saw that the fruit of the tree was good for food and pleasing to the eye, and also desirable for gaining wisdom, she took some and ate it. She also gave some to her husband, who was with her, and he ate it. —Genesis 3:1–6 (NIV)

I struggled with this story every time I heard it, wondering if I were in Eve's place and God gave me a direct and simple command, would I fail? Would I have made the same mistake? Would I have listened to the serpent? "Come on Eve! It is one fruit; how hard is it to find a different fruit in a paradise garden?"

Satan is the most clever and sneaky force, and since the beginning, he has been out to destroy humans. This destruction is caused by three uniquely crafted tactics: doubt, self-righteousness, and fear. In this story, we are introduced to one of his tactics that slides in unnoticed—doubt. Satan questioned God's direct instructions by saying, "Did God really say . . . ?"

When this happened, Eve responded with the Lord's instructions—with a few extra details. Satan had put the question in Eve's mind, and he went in for the counter attack. He provided the thought that maybe God's instructions were not the whole, clear picture and that maybe Eve was missing something. He continued by showing them what earthly knowledge they could possess by eating the fruit.

Eve was hooked and delighted by what she saw and wanted more. That was and is the falling of humans.

Questioning the intentions or the plans of the Lord causes doubt. Satan knows human nature. He uses emotions, curiosity, and deceit to trap us. He does not want you to think anything is wrong with what you are doing. Once this sank into my heart, I recognized that doubt was one of the leading tactics I was falling into every day, and it was the same hidden trap that Eve fell into at the Garden of Eden.

God had given me a direct instruction.

Waiting is not the direction He gives everyone who battles infertility. Some get a yes, a no, or even a wait, but their wait may involve medical interventions or treatments. Mine was a clear and solid "Wait."

Enter stage right, Satan. Did God *really* say wait? All it took for me was one question of God's instruction, and my mind drifted to, *Maybe I misunderstood the Lord's word; maybe I misheard Him or maybe that was not really Him who gave me the answer to wait.*

Just like that, I doubted the direct instructions that I had received.

Once the doubt set in about the Lord's instructions, Satan used his second tactic, introducing self-righteousness to me. I started to entertain the idea that I could grasp the gift of a new baby all on my own. I did not need to wait.

Now, I was unnoticeably stuck in the trap that Satan had set for me. The options and the research that I could do in a matter of minutes were endless, thanks to the internet. I would be consumed by all the options that I had to fix-it-myself. *Maybe He did want me to seek medical interventions; this one lady just got pregnant by taking these vitamins. People say that sex in the morning is best for conceiving. Kyle drinks a lot of soda; maybe putting restrictions on our diet or caffeine is the answer. Maybe I need to get my blood just checked. Maybe I could look into the medical treatments through infertility specialists.*

There were so many options for me . . . right? Any progress towards having a child would make me feel better than just waiting. These thoughts led me down the road of maybe. *Maybe just maybe, God was waiting on me to do some of these things. Maybe I was missing out on the chance of being a mother because I was not taking these steps. Maybe I could have been holding a baby a long time ago. Maybe God is not telling me or showing me everything.*

Now that I was doubting the Lord's plan, trying to achieve it myself, in came Satan's third tactic: fear. Overwhelmed by my options, I started to become afraid. *What if this does not work? What if I never have a child? What if I have this pit of loneliness forever and the desire for a child, but the Lord does not answer?*

Satan got me exactly where he wanted me. I was isolated,

fearful, and doubting that the Lord would be faithful to His word.

Eve fell short to the very first spiritual battle. Would she follow the Lord or would she follow her flesh?

Those who live according to the flesh have their minds set on what the flesh desires; but those who live in accordance with the Spirit have their minds set on what the Spirit desires. The mind governed by the flesh is death, but the mind governed by the Spirit is life and peace. The mind governed by the flesh is hostile to God; it does not submit to God's law, nor can it do so. Those who are in the realm of the flesh cannot please God. —Romans 8:5-8 (NIV)

As followers of Christ, we are called to live by the Spirit, which is the part of God that dwells inside of us. The Spirit navigates us and reveals things in our life, leading us to be like Christ. The flesh is of the evil one. It is all things of this world, desires, and cultures that pull our focus from Christ and puts it on our life and self now. If I am focusing on the flesh, then I am not focusing on Christ. I cannot do both, and Satan wants to do whatever he can to make us live and focus on our flesh.

I was willing to do whatever I could to escape the fear of not being able to have a child. If Satan trap you, you will grasp for anything you can to prevent death, pain, and sorrow. For example, our culture is so scared of death that even the signs of aging such as wrinkles, aches, or changes in the body cause us to seek remedies to preserve the here and now for as long as possible.

My actions when responding to fear are always flesh-focused and not God-focused. I am focused on desires, emotions, anxiety, and desperation so much that I become a slave to them. Satan uses anything in your life to grow that fear, because he knows you cannot serve two masters.

I became a slave to fear of not having a child to hold. I became desperate, and it changed me. The beauty of this trap, though, is that God has already set you free from this slavery and these fears, if you focus on Him. If you are truly focusing on Christ, you cannot focus on the flesh. The Holy Spirit will continue to shape and grow your spirit to become stronger and more mature:

"Since then, you have been raised with Christ, set your hearts on things above, where Christ is, seated at the right hand of God. Set your minds on things above, not on earthly things. For you died, and your life is now hidden with Christ in God" (Colossians 3:1–3).

Spiritual warfare is the battle of my mind, my focus, my heart, and even my time. Some days I do not pay attention to what my mind is on or what I do with my time; my emotions are sporadic and my focus is on the day or minute at hand. On these days I tend to drift without recognizing the battle I am facing and subconsciously losing.

Then randomly, I will have days when I am out of control, feel far from God, and am acting out of my flesh. I should be guarding every thought, questioning every emotion, but instead they move swiftly by without notice. Once the Lord has revealed his instructions to me, it is my job to walk the path that He has directed. God has purpose and a plan for you. He has set you free from all of your forms of slavery:

"Enter through the narrow gate. For wide is the gate and broad is the road that leads to destruction, and many enter through it. But small is the gate and narrow the road that leads to life, and only a few find it" (Matthew 7:13–14).

The evil one has so many schemes and ways into our lives. How do we battle someone we cannot see and who is described as "more crafty than any other beast"? The reason the path to destruction is broad is because it is easy to go down, and there are not many boundaries nor securities. Following the Lord's path is hard, so we find it easy to walk the way of the evil one and let time drift on without taking a step on the path of the Lord.

The path of destruction tends to run with the way of the culture and can be easy to fall into. This path will ultimately lead to destruction. How do I fight this battle? How do I take notice of these everyday emotions, desires, wants and questions that are enslaving me?

In Ephesians 6:10–18 we are given our answer:

Finally, be strong in the Lord and in his mighty power. Put on the full armor of God, so that you can take your stand against the devil's schemes. For our struggle is not against flesh and blood, but against the rulers, against the authorities, against the powers of this dark world and against the spiritual forces of evil in the heavenly realms. Therefore put on the full armor of God, so that when the day of evil comes, you may be able to stand your ground, and after you have done everything, to stand. Stand firm then, with the belt of truth buckled around your waist, with the breastplate of righteousness in place, and with your feet fitted with the readiness that comes from the gospel of peace. In addition to all this, take up the shield of faith, with which you can extinguish all the flaming arrows of the evil one. Take the helmet of salvation and the sword of the Spirit, which is the word of God.

And pray in the Spirit on all occasions with all kinds of prayers and requests. With this in mind, be alert and always keep on praying for all the Lord's people.

—Ephesians 6:10–18

The armor of God is wrapped around us. Into battle we go!

All these pieces of armor hypothetically sound good, but what do they actually mean and instruct us to do? We will work through each part of the armor and how to prepare for battle with each piece of armor.

In a suit of armor, there can be areas of weakness or vulnerability—this is often called a chink in the armor. In each part of the spiritual armor of God that I would put on, I had chinks. If I was not careful, Satan would take advantage of my weakness and focus my attention back on my flesh and fear.

Belt of Truth

Stand firm then, with the belt of truth buckled around your waist . . . (v. 14)

A few types of belts have been found on armor over time. One is the kind that latches all of the armor onto the body. You are able to tighten the belt and buckle around the arm, to make it snug, and fit the body appropriately. The other type of belt goes around the waist and holds the sword and the armor together.

Just like the armor, two truths go into the "Belt of Truth." The first truth is the truth of God, which holds all the other armor on and in place. If you had to answer the question, "Who is God?" or "Who is Jesus Christ?" what would you say? Would you say you believe He is the Creator of the universe? That He is the God of the past, present, and the future? That He sent His Son to save us so we can spend eternity worshiping and glorifying Him?

Would you say that He has a purpose for you in this life and in eternity? Who do you say He is? God is the truth, God is life, and God is above all. Here are some scriptures that tell us about who He is.

- *Revelation 22:13, "I am the Alpha and the Omega, the first and the last, the beginning and the end."*
- *Colossians 1:16: "For by him all things were created, in heaven and on earth, visible and invisible, whether thrones or dominions or rulers or authorities—all things were created through him and for him."*

• *John 3:16: "For God so loved the world, that he gave his only Son, that whoever believes in him should not perish but have eternal life."*

• *Jeremiah 29:11: "For I know the plans I have for you, declares the Lord, plans of good and not for evil, to give you a future and a hope."*

The second type of belt is worn on the waist and can hold weapons, armor, and patriotic symbols. This belt always points in the direction that you are going. This type of belt represents the truth of who you are and who you are in Christ.

Many people, including myself, struggle with our identity. I struggled with the identity that I desired on this earth in comparison to whom God called me to be at this specific time in my life. I wanted the identity of a mother, of a caregiver. I would often feel discouraged by the identities that I did not fit into, as opposed to the ones that I was and could claim.

Whether or not I would ever become a mother, I held the same identity to God. My identity in Christ should overshadow any other identity that I desire. Who am I to God? Who are you to God? What is your identity?

• *Galatians 2:20: "I have been crucified with Christ. It is no longer I who live, but Christ who lives in me. And the life I now live in the flesh I live by faith in the Son of God, who loved me and gave himself for me. "*

• *John 1:12: "But to all who did receive him, who believed in his name, he gave the right to become children of God."*

• *Ephesians 2:10: "For we are his workmanship, created in Christ Jesus for good works, which God prepared beforehand, that we should walk in them."*

• *1 Peter 2:9: "But you are a chosen race, a royal priesthood, a holy nation, a people of his own possession, that you may proclaim the excellencies of him who called you out of darkness into his marvelous light."*

• *John 15:5: "I am the vine; you are the branches. Whoever abides in me and I in him, he is to bear much fruit, for apart from me you can do nothing."*

I am loved by God. I am a child of God. He has designed me the way that I am for good, not evil. He wants me to use my life to glorify him. He will guide me, prepare me, grow me, and comfort me. Am I seeking that as my identity, or am I clinging to an identity that I want and see in other people?

This world defines identity as multiple pieces that make up a puzzle of the person you are. Different pieces are represented as categories, such as physical appearance, talents, abilities, race, culture, gender, defining moments, experiences, jobs, beliefs, relationships, and so on. The feel-good part about this view of identity is that if you like all the pieces of your life and are successful, then you feel confident and proud of whom you are. However, if you have defining moments that are negative memories, or are not happy or content with your circumstances, then you come to a point where you have missing pieces and the whole puzzle crumbles.

For example, if you are in a relationship that is key part of your life and it falls apart, you feel as if you have lost part of who you are. Now, you pull on other areas of your life to fill that empty spot. Unfortunately, the next piece may not fit exactly right and you are left with a hole needing to be filled. Your identity starts to crumble, you feel lost, and you do not know who you truly are.

A different view of your identity is illustrated by a vine. When I choose to follow Christ, He becomes my vine and my identity is the branch. Every leaf or fruit that is produced is filtered and nourished by Christ. On a vine, you have branches, and those branches have leaves that make this branch special. The purpose of the branch is to produce fruit. If the

branch does not get nourishment from the vine, it cannot produce leaves and vines, and the branch will wither away. The Bible talks about this concept in John 15:

"I am the vine; you are the branches. Whoever abides in me and I in him, he is to bear much fruit, for apart from me you can do nothing. If anyone does not remain in me, he is like a branch that is thrown away and withers" (John 15:5).

Every part of our identity is filtered through Christ and is sustained, only to flourish with the Lord's will. This takes all the weight off our shoulders, because our identity is in Christ and not in our accomplishments, successes, or failures. We do not have to have shame in the areas of our life that are harder or different than others because we can be secure in knowing that Christ has a part in each segment of our identity. When we feel insecure or unsure of what should be doing and who we are, we need to fall back into the vine that nourishes us.

This concept that every part of us stems from and through Christ is much different than the worldly view. Instead of your beliefs just being one part of the puzzle, every portion of your life depends on Christ. For example, every relationship I have should be sustained and full of love that I show from Christ. My appearance should not be about comparing myself to others but to focusing on how Christ views me, designed me, and created me. No matter the imperfections or faults I find, I am fearfully and wonderfully made the way I am for a reason that only Christ knows.

I have a passion for teaching; God gave me that gift and talents to be used for His glory. He gives me jobs and experiences to share His love and spread the good news of the grace that He alone offers. My branch is full of leaves: wife; teacher;

photographer; writer; memories and experiences that made me grow, gave me heartaches, and allowed wonderful celebrations.

However, one leaf that I desired to possess would not grow. The leaf of motherhood was an identity I strove for, and I envied other women. I would pray to the Lord to let this leaf be part of my branch, but it would never grow. This was a weakness to me. I viewed my identity as less than others because I was without the leaf of a child.

My mindset needs to change. I am not *missing* a leaf. God did not make a mistake. Instead of my leaf saying "child," it said "infertile." This was a hard leaf to want or even come to grips that I possessed, but God had nourished and prepared me for this leaf. He is using it, and if I fall back into Him, knowing that He has prepared me and designed me with this leaf in mind, He will use it to grow fruit. If my mindset does not change, I will miss opportunities that God is trying to use me for.

We continually ask God to fill you with the knowledge of his will through all the wisdom and understanding that the Spirit gives, so that you may live a life worthy of the Lord and please him in every way: bearing fruit in every good work, growing in the knowledge of God, being strengthened with all power according to his glorious might so that you may have great endurance and patience, and giving joyful thanks to the Father, who has qualified you to share in the inheritance of his holy people in the kingdom of light. For he has rescued us from the dominion of darkness and brought us into the kingdom of the Son he loves, in whom we have redemption, the forgiveness of sins.

—Colossians 3:9–14

Our branch is our identity that relies on the nourishment of Jesus Christ. Our identity can point towards who Christ is, or it can point away from him. When you *put on* the belt of truth, you are putting aside those distractions and lies Satan is trying to use.

With those lies, he is trying to change your focus from being on who God is and who He has created you to be to what is missing in this life. Stand firm in your decision to follow Christ and fight the evil one. Do not waver from His instructions. He will not let you miss His plan for you!

Questions for Reflection:

Who is God to you?

____

____

Who are you to Christ?

____

____

What would be leaves on your branch?

____

____

Are there any leaves that you desperately want but do not possess?

____

____

What are some ways you feel that God is using you exactly where you are?

____

____

Breastplate of Righteousness

. . . with the breastplate of righteousness in place (v. 14)

The largest piece of armor on a warrior is the breastplate. The breastplate covers the chest, to protect vital organs that keep the body alive, mainly the heart. According to *Healthline,* the human heart beats an average of 115,000 times per day. It takes about 45 seconds for the heart to circulate blood out to all parts of the body and return to the heart. With every beat, there is a sense of frailty. There is no room for error because any clot, valve leak, or misread signal could have a fatal outcome.

The heart is what keeps our flesh healthy physically, but it is also what keeps us alive spiritually. The spiritual heart has been known as the seat for affections or our source of being, emotions, and sensibility. Just like catastrophic things can happen to our heart, damage to our spiritual heart can cause us to be hardened, numb, and act in ways that may harm others and ourselves.

Emotions, in themselves, are not bad. In fact, they are essential to our survival. For example, the emotion of enjoyment allows your body to relax, feel secure, and connect with people around you. Sadness and tears allow your body to release toxins and provide endorphins to momentarily numb the pain. Fear protects you from harmful situations and provides balance in an area or time of uncertainty. We tend to view anger as a negative emotion, but it allows for opportunities of optimism, problem solving, and it alerts others that something is wrong to provoke a conversation. All these emotions have their times and places, and are felt regularly. You can probably identify when you have experienced one, if not all of these emotions in the last twenty-four hours. Emotions are normal and are part of who we humans are.

The tricky part with emotions, and the reason that our hearts are easily seduced, is because there is not a distinct line between when emotions are healthy and when they are being twisted and used by Satan. When left unchecked, our emotions can cloud our conscience to the point that we lose our ability to discern guidance from God through the Holy Spirit. As a result, we act out or behave in ways that are controlled by our emotions, our flesh, and Satan—and not by the spirit. There is a constant battle happening for the control of the heart, and emotions are the key.

On the night that Jesus was betrayed, the guards came to arrest him. Several of His disciples were with Him, and Jesus had told His disciples many times before that this betrayal was necessary for the promise to be fulfilled. One of the disciples, Peter, drew his sword and sliced off the servant's ear when the guards came to arrest Jesus. Peter acted out viciously and was controlled by his emotions, not by the guidance of Jesus who was standing beside him. Perhaps Peter felt his duty was to protect his "Rabbi," the teacher Peter had dedicated his life to follow. Maybe Peter's reality was suddenly threatened by the men who came to take Jesus away. Whatever the exact reasoning, it appears Peter's emotions overtook him; and he was prepared to fight.

On those days when I saw those negative pregnancy tests, my emotions would overcome me. I would make mean comments to people who were closest to me or even innocent bystanders who had nothing to do with my daily life. I spent hours in tears and looked in spite at women who had what I wanted. When my flesh and emotions were in control, instead of being used as a communication tool, my anger was directed at God for His plan, and I would then take it out on others. The feeling of sadness would expand to the deep pit of my stomach. I would feel hopeless, fearing that my desire for a child would never come true, and I would never be satisfied.

My emotions led me to self-indulgence of food and other desires, simply because I felt as though my enjoyment was not being met and was outside of my control. Food and other consumables were something that I could control and could have without being told, "No."

Fear was the worst for me. When the sense of fear started to gain control, I would be overwhelmed by the thoughts that I would not ever have children and that I needed to do something about that—right now! I needed to pursue the desire for children beyond what the Lord had told me to do. I needed to do it my way, right now, because I was running out of time.

I could feel fear creeping up into my throat, like I was centimeters away from drowning. I was gripping and grasping for my own answer, in my own way. I wanted my life to go the way that I wanted. In these moments of suffocating in my own fear, I would close my fist around the desire to have a child, in hopes that God would see how tightly and precious this desire was for me. I would cry out to Him, hoping God heard my cries, saying, "You can have everything else but not this; not this one desire I have dreamed of since a young age." My spirit was no longer in control.

Emotions are a slippery slope. They are an easy way for Satan to overtake our flesh for brief instances that can be damaging to ourselves and others. In the moment that Peter reached out and sliced off a guard's ear, Jesus reprimanded him. Although Peter could not take back his action, he put his sword back in the sheath. Jesus took the servant and healed his ear.

Jesus had told the disciples previously that this was His purpose for being on the earth. Yet, Peter still acted, probably out of emotion, against God's plan. Jesus's reaction of healing the servant was a way to show that no human act could stand in the way of His plan happening as it was intended. Had Jesus left the soldier's ear damaged, Jesus could possibly have been held responsible for Peter's action since Peter was Jesus's disciple. That was apparently not in the plan, and he healed the servant.

God's plan would then fulfill the Scriptures. There was no way for Peter to stop, alter, or change the plan of Jesus dying a specific death in the way that God had intended it.

When I act in fear, anger, lash out to others, or even take steps in a way that tries to force God's hand into accomplishing my desire, I only distract myself. I distract myself from taking steps of obedience and miss opportunities to turn the glory back to God. As I stand there, lost in my emotions with my fist closed tightly, God, in His sovereignty, does not just leave me but pursues me. He softens my spirit through scriptures, songs, and His people. I then feel my fist loosen, and I am left feeling remorse for the anger I had against the Lord. God so graciously reminds me of His plan, purpose, and my ultimate goal of using my life to honor Him.

Every part of my life should be an open palm to the Lord for Him to take and use for His glory, not mine. My whole life is in his hands, and I lay my life back at His feet on that cross. He creates a barrier that protects my heart and guards my emotions in the form of the breastplate of righteousness. I cannot get the righteousness on my own, but only through Christ's death on the cross and the perfect life that He lived. When I am imperfect, God will pick me up and surround my body in protection against the evil one.

Questions for Reflection:

Are you experiencing emotions that distract you from taking steps of obedience?

____

____

Have you had instances in the past that you need to apologize for because you were controlled by emotions?

____

____

What emotion do you tend to fall prey to the most?

____

____

Do your actions line up with God's plan, or are they based on uncontrolled emotions?

____

____

What do you hold onto so tightly?

____

____

Sword of the Spirit

. . . And the sword of the Spirit, which is the word of God. (Ephesians 6:17)

Hearing the words "*sword of the spirit*" provokes an image from my childhood—a soldier with a long silver sword and, at the end, a handle engraved with intricate gold details. This sword was known by enemies and was regarded fiercely. When held at rest, it was stored in a gold sheath on a leather belt around the soldier's waist.

Although the image still rings true in my head, the meaning behind the sword has changed. The sword of the Spirit is also known as the Word of God or Holy Bible. The Bible is our offensive and defensive weapon to the world we live in. It reveals to us the different characteristics of God through the lives and stories of men and women, including His own son, Jesus Christ. The Word gives us wisdom in situations and Christ's strength when our backs are against the wall. It shows us guidance in our everyday mundane lives, and in times when we feel surrounded by enemies the Word reminds us that Christ is surrounding us.

How can one book give us each the guidance we need through completely different situations, circumstances, and questions? Have you ever realized when multiple people read the same story from the Bible, their takeaways are completely different and certain details standout while others remain hidden? As we read the Bible, each word is translated through our Holy Spirit, who takes the words on the page and gives us insight into our own lives. This gives us the ability to communicate and hear straight from the Lord and His intentions for us.

For the word of God is alive and active. Sharper than any double-edged sword, it penetrates even to dividing soul and spirit, joints and

marrow; it judges the thoughts and attitudes of the heart. Nothing in all creation is hidden from God's sight. Everything is uncovered and laid bare before the eyes of him to whom we must give account.
—Hebrews 4:12–13

The sword separates the joints and marrow from the soul and spirit. This visual speaks to the Bible's ability to discern the motive of an action as from the flesh or from the spirit. Your spirit will seek to grow and mature to be more like Christ while your flesh will seek opportunities to make the most of this life through pleasures of the heart.

As we live every day, we face obstacles and hills. There are so many paths to get through them that it is hard to discern the obedient route. Our world would tell us to follow whatever route we can to get what we desire. Yet, that is not what God tells us to do. He gives us one path of guidance and direction. A failure to follow that direction is sinful.

This creates a problem for me. When I asked for a family, God's response was *"wait."* Nothing more, just wait. As I sat and waited, my urge to have children strengthened. I watched other women around me have children. I viewed it as an achievement, not a gift. I wanted a child. Women around me took steps to achieve their desire for children. They would seek the Lord, and He would open the paths that led to doctor visits, surgeries, solutions and plans.

The idea of seeking answers and solutions appealed to me. I wanted it so bad, but something held me back. I felt uneasiness, anxiousness, and as though I were trying to get in a house that did not belong to me. Why did I feel that? It was not wrong for other women to invest in answers, doctors, and procedures. Why was it wrong for me?

So is my word that goes out from my mouth: It will not return to me empty, but will accomplish what I desire and achieve the purpose for which I sent it. —Isaiah 55:11

The internal warfare I faced was due to the instructions that I had received from the Lord. God had told me to wait. The Bible discerns the heart behind each action and thought. The Holy Spirit bring light to the motives that are flesh-focused. When I started to feel guilty about the things I was doing, it was because I was acting in disobedience. This was the Holy Spirit trying to correct and guide me. At times I would ignore this feeling. The desire to have children would overrule the desire to grow to be like Christ. I would start to seek advice and empowerment from other people so I would feel like my actions were right and obedient. Honestly, the truth only comes from God who speaks directly to us through the Bible. And my actions were not of that truth.

The sword of the spirit is there to discern God's purpose for me and His plan that is being played out before my eyes. God's saying, "Wait" can feel like torture or like it is meant to just prevent me from getting what I want, but it is not.

As followers of Christ, we commit our lives to live for His purpose and not our own, with eyes for eternity and not the pleasures of this world. Even if He does not give me what I want, He will satisfy me in all that I do because Jesus is greater than anything I could have or hold in this life. He will lift me up, guide me and protect me in the shadow of His wing. The sword of the Spirit releases us from the ropes that tie us to this world, and though that process may hurt, God gave us his book of promises to cling to, write, read, scream, pray and weep over as we fight off our enemies. He promises to walk by our side, lead us and give us joy and wisdom even in the darkest of times. He is there. Open his word and find Him. Find His discernment for your life.

Questions for Reflection:

Do you spend time in the word?

____

____

How do you take time to hear from God?

____

____

Do you spend time listening?

____

____

What hard questions do you want to ask God but are scared to hear the answers to?

____

____

In what ways have you been obedient?

____

____

Do you find yourself seeking empowerment from people, or do you feel at peace?

____

____

Challenge:

Of the scriptures that have been noted in this book, select one that holds on to you and memorize it.

____

____

Shoes of Peace

And with your feet fitted with the readiness that comes from the gospel of peace (v. 15).

In biblical times, Roman soldiers wore sandals that were fastened with tough leather for stability. Nails on the bottom of the soles helped the shoes withstand long marches and could also be used as a weapon if necessary. Even though we do not wear Roman combat shoes today, shoes still have basically the same function. They are meant to support the foot through different terrains to allow a person to get to his or her destination.

As we walk our journey, our purpose is to carry the gospel, also known as the good news, which is the news of Jesus Christ, and share it with people everywhere we go. God has put us on a path where we will encounter people who are unique to our specific journey. Some people who cross our path may be there only briefly, while others are walking alongside us for long distances.

Even if our paths align with each other, we come from different starting points, carry different weights, and have different aches, pains, and hopes. These differences are what make our meetings and relationship with them so beautifully unique. So, what is our purpose for having relationships with people? Why do we run into people and it seems like our meeting is not just chance? What do we do with these opportunities?

"Go therefore and make disciples of all nations, baptizing them in the name of the Father and of the Son and of the Holy Spirit, teaching them to observe all that I have commanded you. And behold, I am with you always, to the end of the age." —Matthew 28:19–20

Our purpose is so clearly laid out in these verses of Matthew.

We are to go spread the news of Jesus Christ to all people, all the time. God gave us a specific story. The things that have happened to you or choices you have had to make are unique. God has designed and used all the decisions in your life to create a unique story that is meant to bring glory to His name. You are able to relate and connect to people who are in the same battle as you—especially when you are seeking answers. You can show others how God showed up in your battle and was with you. He may not have answered the questions as you would have liked or given you the dream you want, but you can speak of true hope—hope that will never fail and is beyond any answer of this world. You can share the gospel of Jesus Christ.

My message and my preaching were not with wise and persuasive words, but with a demonstration of the spirit's power, so that your faith might not rest on human wisdom, but on God's power. —1 Corinthians 2:4–5

When I think about sharing the gospel, I lean toward John 3:16 or the Roman Road. Although those are wonderful ways to grasp and understand the good news, they are not the only way to share the gospel. I sometimes feel as though I will fail when sharing the gospel, that I will not remember the right passage or say the right words.

The Bible reminds us over and over again that human words do not bring people to faith in Jesus Christ; that is a result of God's almighty power. Knowing that relieves the pressure from our shoulders. We do not have to create a cookie cutter script of what to say while waiting for someone to ask us the specific question: "Will you share the gospel with me?" Instead, we can share about the power of God that we see in our own lives.

How God has shown up for you and been present in your circumstances? Dark times are when Christ's light shines the brightest. At times it is hard to share, or you are in a situation that leaves you feeling that the last thing you want to do is share the Word of God. But these are the times when people need to see the light of God. This does not mean you have to be happy and perky, but ask God in the moments that are hard, *how do You want to use this? Who are* you *trying to reach?*

God will guide your steps and bring you opportunities to share his light. The beauty of wearing shoes of the gospel, it that the shoes carry you everywhere you go—in a hospital room, crashed on the bathroom floor, at a restaurant, or even in your home. You can and are instructed to spread the love of Jesus Christ wherever you are. He will guide each step you need to take. He will overwhelm you with a peace that surpasses all understanding. He will comfort you and encourage you. He will guide your words. He will always be with you, to the end of the age.

Many people believe techniques like meditation, calming the mind, doing good things, or just choosing your thoughts will bring you peace. Although these strategies are good to practice, they will not give you true peace. According to a website, Faith Hope and Love, "Peace is more than just the absence of conflict; it means completeness, wholeness and lacking nothing." (www.wordsoffaithhopelove.com)

It is not possible for unbelievers to fully experience peace, because they cannot be complete or whole without Christ. Jesus Christ was also referred to as the Prince of Peace:

"For to us a child is born, to us a son is given; and the government shall be upon his shoulder and his name shall be called Wonderful Counselor, Mighty God, Everlasting Father, Prince of Peace" (Isaiah 9:6).

When we ask the Prince of Peace, He gives us peace that

surpasses all understanding. In times of trial and hardship, He will provide a sense of comfort and protection. God will not always take away the pain but He will fill us with His peace and remind us who is ultimately in control.

Spiritual warfare is happening all the time. People are always under attack from Satan. Satan uses people like pawns; he is behind much of the sin and terrible things that happen in this life. He is also the force behind anxious thoughts, worries, or concerns. Alone, you cannot fight off these conflicts, but if you have faith in Jesus Christ, you have the Holy Spirit to guide you through these times and give you peace that fills beyond what anything in this world can do.

Therefore, since we have been justified by faith, we have peace with God through our Lord Jesus Christ. —Romans 5:1

An unbeliever does not have the Holy Spirit; therefore, the conflict will never cease and there is not hope. Unbelievers will never have true peace. Because of this, we believers stand out in times of conflict because we have complete peace and give the conflict back to the Lord to fight the battles in our place. We become instruments that are used and guided, instead of taking on the attacks of the enemies. God becomes our defender.

God uses these times in our lives—times of heart aches and uncertainty. We know that even if everything on this earth will fade and end, He will not. He will hold on to us in the palm of His hands. If we are willing in times of hardships to lift our eyes to what He is doing, God will use these hardships in our lives to bring others to Him. We just have to be willing to let go of our wants, frustrations and plans and cling to Him for the peace that only He can provide.

Do not be anxious about anything, but in everything by prayer and supplication with thanksgiving let your requests be made known to God. And the peace of God, which surpasses all understanding, will guard your hearts and your minds in Christ Jesus. —Philippians 4:6–7

"I have said these things to you, that in me you may have peace. In the world you will have tribulation. But take heart; I have overcome the world." —John 16:33

Our journeys can be long and, like the Roman soldiers, we could endure long marches that require support and stability on our feet to keep us going. Only God provides us with the exact shoes we need to be successful. He provides us support through His Word and the body of Christ; He provides endurance so our feet do not wear out. He provides peace and a gospel message to spread, as we go about sharing the good news of Jesus Christ and the power of God.

Questions for Reflection:

Have you felt God's incomprehensible peace? Do you need to ask Him for it?

___

___

Think of your journey right now—who might God want you to reach out to?

___

___

What are dreams, wants or achievements do you desire to have in this life?

___

___

What motivates you to accomplish these dreams, wants, achievements?

___

___

In what ways are you using your wants, desires, and accomplishments in this life to glorify the Lord?

___

___

How can you use your story to show his grace and salvation?

___

___

Helmet of Salvation

Take the helmet of salvation (v. 17),

When you think about a great warrior, who comes to mind? Maybe you think of Alexander the Great, who conquered Persia, Egypt, and surrounding areas. Maybe you think of the Spartan warriors who dedicated their lives to training so that they could defend enemies to protect their country. Or maybe you think of our everyday heroes who lay down their lives for our freedom.

All these kinds of warriors deserve our respect, whether you fight on the same side as them or not. But why? What makes them so great?

These warriors have "fight" in their eyes with nothing to lose and everything to gain. This is what makes them so dangerous! They are willing to do whatever it costs—even lay down their own lives—for a bigger purpose.

As Christ followers, you have put your faith in Jesus Christ and have received salvation. Salvation is deliverance from eternal damnation to, instead, spend eternity with Jesus Christ. He has come, conquered sin, and risen from the grave. He has forgiven all sins of yesterday, today, and tomorrow, but you have to accept His free gift.

You have been told that whatever happens in this world, if all you cherish falls away and the world disintegrates, your salvation will still stand. No matter what conflict, temptation or situation you face, your eternity cannot be taken away by any acts from this physical Earth or by Satan himself. You can have confidence, freedom from the possibility of your dreams not coming true, fear of losing or failing because you hold the promise of salvation and that can not be taken from you:

"For God so loved the world, that he gave his only Son, that whoever believes in him should not perish but have eternal life" (John 3:16).

Salvation is the truth that God sent his only Son to die for you. He took away all your sin and gave you a new spirit. While you live in this world, and continue to sin, Christ has covered all your past, current, and future sins so you can spend an eternity with him. Salvation is not something that you have to earn or be good enough for; it is a gift from God to all His children. The truth is, you will never be good enough. Once we are saved, we change our focus from the material things and desires of this world, to put our focus on God's desires and plans. Scripture gives us guidance that speaks to our spirit and molds us to be like Christ. Salvation is talked about as a helmet because it guards and focuses the mind.

For me, this was a struggle. I wanted to hold on to the life that I wanted, the American dream, plus I had salvation. I wanted the best life now and also in eternity. I would hold on so tightly and close my fist around the plan to have a family and children. That is like a soldier who wants to be a good warrior with nothing to lose, but also wants to hold onto his or her life and plans outside of the current fight.

For whoever wants to save their life will lose it, but whoever loses their life for me will find it. —Matthew 16:25

This verse does not encourage the end of your physical life, but speaks of your giving your life, decisions, plans, and desires over to God. He will give you a life greater than this one. Scripture shows us two men who illustrated this choice well. Genesis tells us about a man named Abram, who God promised to be the father of many nations. Abram was directed to leave his homeland and wealth and to live as a foreigner in a land that would someday be filled with his descendants. Abram took his nephew, Lot, with him.

Lot also believed and followed God but at one point, due to conflict, Abram and Lot had to go separate ways. Abram let Lot choose to go left or right, and he would then go the opposite way:

Then Abram said to Lot, "Let there be no strife between you and me, and between your herdsmen and my herdsmen, for we are kinsmen. Is not the whole land before you? Separate yourself from me. If you take the left hand, then I will go to the right, or if you take the right hand, then I will go to the left." And Lot lifted up his eyes and saw that the Jordan Valley was well watered everywhere like the garden of the Lord, like the land of Egypt, in the direction of Zoar. (This was before the Lord destroyed Sodom and Gomorrah.) So, Lot chose for himself all the Jordan Valley, and Lot journeyed east. Thus, they separated from each other. Abram settled in the land of Canaan, while Lot settled among the cities of the valley and moved his tent as far as Sodom. Now the men of Sodom were wicked, great sinners against the Lord (Genesis 13:8–13).

Lot chose to hold on to the desires of this world. He knew that area of Egypt was corrupt with people who served different gods and were led by their own desires. These towns were wicked and full of sin. Verse eleven says Lot "lifted up his eyes," which signals that Lot willingly chose to satisfy the desires of his life at that point; he wanted instant gratification in his wealth and wanted to live his best life then. As time went on, we know that Sodom and Gomorrah, the cities in the Jordan valley, where Lot chose to live, were destroyed due to the wickedness of the people there. Lot, in the process, lost his wife and possessions. This story speaks another meaning to the verse in Matthew 10:39 (NKJV), *"He who saves his life will lose it."*

Lot desired the more beautiful and comfortable place to live, but God, in His divine judgment and working in His own plan, took an action that meant Lot lost his home. Perhaps Lot learned, as a result, that eternity is all that matters.

Abram responded in a different manner after he separated from Lot: "The Lord said to Abram, after Lot had separated from him, 'Lift up your eyes and look from the place where you are, northward and southward and eastward and westward, for all the land that you see I will give to you and to your offspring forever. I will make your offspring as the dust of the earth, so that if one can count the dust of the earth, your offspring also can be counted. Arise, walk through the length and the breadth of the land, for I will give it to you'" (Genesis 13:14–17).

Abram had nothing to hold on to, nothing to cherish over the Lord. He gave it all to the Lord. Abram allowed the Lord to lift up his eyes and direct his steps. The Lord not only guided him but also gave Abram a blessing that he would receive in full during eternity with Christ.

Abram held nothing back from the Lord. Can you imagine what your life would be like if you opened all the doors to your life and laid everything you are and hope to be at the Lord's feet? What would He do? Would you be willing to give up your ideas, plans and desires to say that the only thing that matters to you is salvation with Christ?

If we are being honest, it is scary to lay down all your wants and say above all, "Lord, I want you and your salvation." At times I feel numb to the understanding of salvation. It is easy to shrug and say, "I have salvation, now God, can I have this? God, I want that. I have a desire for this. Please give it to me."

When I follow this pattern, I forget that my whole purpose in life is not to pursue my happiness; it is about a commitment I gave to the Lord as a young kid. God will spend time waking me up from this state of numbness by waiting for me, giving me trials, or adding pressure to areas that I hold onto so I will recognize where my allegiance lies.

Along with forgetting all else and fighting the battle at hand, the best warriors are ones who, without question, follow the instructions of their authorities. They listen to those who lead them. They do not always know what to do, what mission or task to accomplish next, but they have someone in charge to follow. Whether they agree with what they are told or whether or not they want to pay the cost, they trust the authority. When the captain or leader says to stand firm, they do. When their leader tells them to attack, they do. They do not show any distraction of hesitations from their command. They commit their lives and trust that their authority has their best interest at hand for the country and for all the people they serve.

Whatever you do, work heartily, as for the Lord and not for men, knowing that from the Lord you will receive the inheritance as your reward. You are serving the Lord, Jesus Christ. —Colossians 3:23–24

Our culture preaches a different message such as, "YOLO (you only live once) or live your best life today." This world has become filled with self-serving people who need instant gratification in their lives. The purpose of life has become all about making the most for yourself, being the best person you can be, and getting all the things that you want. It is about fulfilling yourself with the desires of this world. It is holding on to salvation and knowing that you will have Christ in eternity, but holding onto all your dreams in this life as well.

You cannot have both. You cannot serve Jesus Christ while also serving yourself. It is not really yourself you are serving, but the traps that Satan has set, and you are serving him.

This is the lie that Lot bought into when he lifted his eyes onto the beauty of the sin-filled valley, and God's divine judgment striped everything from him.

I am not saying we should not enjoy life, but the reason we

do things and the decisions we make should be with the understanding that this is life is going to fulfill all our wants and dreams and to serve and obey God. When my focus is only on myself and what I want, it is me serving Satan and falling trap to his manipulation that this life is as good as it gets. It's God or Satan. If you love Jesus Christ and believe in Him as your Savior, this lifetime is as hard and the worst that it will ever be.

We have a promise that all the pains, hurts, and desires that leave us heartbroken, are chained to this world. When we get to heaven, they will all be gone, and then we will see and glorify God for the rest of eternity.

On the other hand, if you do not love and follow Jesus, this life is the best that you will ever have. The eternity that waits for a non-believer is full of pain and the wrath of God, like displayed at Sodom and Gomorrah.

Serving yourself instead of the Lord is fighting a losing battle. Satan will use any opportunity as a foothold to get into your mind and distract you from the true battle at hand. Remember whom you serve, Jesus Christ. He alone can defeat the attacks of Satan. Let go of all else, so that God may be able to lift your eyes and guide your steps for His glory. When you do, you will feel like a warrior ready to fight the battle at hand. You will put on the helmet of salvation knowing that everything in this world is temporary and all else in this life will fall away except for your salvation in Christ.

Questions for Reflection:

In what ways do you feel as though you are drawn to live your best life now?

____

____

What are areas that you tend to hold on to and become hindrances to letting God lift your eyes?

____

____

In what ways do you let God be your authority, your commander?

____

____

What areas has He guided you to stand firm in, and what areas has he asked you to give to him?

____

____

What ways do you find yourself focusing on this life?

____

____

Is there anything in your past that you feel Satan is using to say that you are undeserving?

____

____

Shield of Faith

Take up the shield of faith, with which you can extinguish all the flaming arrows of the evil one. (v. 16)

In the present day, we tend to see warriors wearing bulletproof vests or clothing that prevents injury, but back in the biblical days, shields were a vital part of defense on the battlefield. They protected the body from arrows or swords intended to harm. When an arrow would come flying from the sky, a warrior would cover his or her entire body and allow the shield to take the impact, having faith that the shield would withstand the strength of the arrow. Until that moment when the arrow impacted the shield, the soldier had faith in the shield to the extent that he placed his body behind that shield. Faith is the assurance in something that is unseen, or has not happened yet.

My husband and I started playing golf this past summer. Between the eighth and ninth holes of our regular course was a deep ravine. You had to cross a bridge with your golf bag to get from one hole to the other. As I was walking across, I felt the bridge give way a little bit, and I looked down to see that the whole bridge was covered in wood rot. It shook with every step I took. I was halfway across the bridge. At this point, I had to have faith—but faith in what?

Just saying I have faith does not make sense; I have to have faith in something or someone. At that moment with every step taken, I revealed faith in the old rickety bridge to hold up as I walked across it. Since I am not one hundred percent sure it will hold me up, I am placing my *faith* in it.

Jesus Christ is the same way. If you believe that God created the universe, you have faith because no one was there to see it. Therefore, you have to have assurance in something that is unseen. If you believe that at the end of all we know, Christ will return and He will ultimately win the battle over evil, you have faith in Jesus Christ and His sovereign will. When you act in faith in Jesus Christ, you are taking a step that you normally would not take because you believe in His plan and the eternity that you will be spending with Him in heaven.

The Bible tells of two things: who God is and people who have acted or refused to act in faith. You read about people like Moses, who delivered the Israelites from slavery in Egypt; Noah who built a boat to save his family and animals from a flood; or Sarah who continued to wait for a child for ninety years. There are even smaller characters who are mentioned in just a few sentences in the Bible. All of these examples took faith, and specifically, faith in Jesus Christ.

You will see two types of faith throughout the Bible and probably throughout your own life as well. There are moments of faith and times of steadfast faith. Moments of faith show up in the Bible in stories like the woman in Matthew 9:20–22 who suffered from a discharge of bleeding for twelve years. She was an outcast and isolated. Then the woman saw Jesus passing and she touched His garment. She had faith that Jesus Christ could heal her, and that is exactly what happened. A more common moment of faith was of David, a shepherd boy, who went to fight a giant, Goliath, and came out victorious with only a slingshot and a stone. The Bible also shows us times of steadfast faith like Noah who was instructed to build a boat, which might have taken up to a 100-year period. He followed in dedication to the Lord even while being mocked and ridiculed for building a boat. Sarah was told that she would conceive a child and after years of following the Lord, she was given a son at age ninety.

As you read through the Bible, you see ordinary people who were called to stand out in moments of faith. In each story, obstacles were put in the way for each person. Even then it was

Satan trying to break down their shield of faith. Moses was mocked and made into a joke by the people around him. Sarah started to doubt that God would come through and had Abraham conceive a child with her handmaiden. The woman who bled for twelve years was probably forced into isolation for years because she was considered unclean and possibly thought not worthy to be near others.

Obstacles we see in the Bible and challenges that we face are designed to try our allegiance to Christ, His plan, and goodness. At the same time, Satan is there, firing his arrows of temptations, distractions, and rejections to remind us that we are not for this world.

As I look back on my journey, I see so many moments of faith, and as I wait on the Lord, I feel the weight of the steadfast faith. Along with those times that I felt comforted by the perseverance that I was given, I also saw times where I stood outside of the shield of faith, and was hit with arrows of distractions and temptations. I missed out on opportunities to have moments of faith or show the steadfast faith I have in the Lord.

I have times when I felt like I should say something or pray for someone, but an anxious feeling comes over me, and I worry about the awkwardness that could arise. Will people think I am weird or could this ruin a friendship?

Or in steadfast faith, time can allow for doubt to creep in. Even people with good intentions can be discouraging to your long-time act of faith and create a sense of uncertainty.

We have been waiting for a child for almost five years and many times I have felt jealousy creep in when I've seen a mother with her child. My faith would start to dwindle, and doubt and anger would try to claw their way into my life.

I started to focus on things like age. *What if I get too old to have a child? The normal thing to do is to get married and have kids.* You can see all the arrows that Satan sends our way, such as *you are not good enough* or *your past defines you* or *you will never get pregnant.* He will do anything to discourage you and change the focus to the desires at hand instead of keeping your thoughts on Christ and the plan to glorify Him. I cannot tell you how many times that I have been convinced that I would not have a child due to shameful ways I used my body and my poor decisions with men in my young adult years. Thoughts like, *I would never have a child because I do not deserve to have a child* or *This is payback for all the bad things I have done.*

LIES! That is Satan changing the focus. I have been forgiven. I am not saying I do not face consequences for my wrong behaviors, but that is not the explanation for my infertility. That tactic is all lies and Satan steering my eyes away from the faith that I have in Jesus Christ.

The shield is a defensive weapon that is meant to protect. In the same way, we have to know *when* to draw near and behind the shield of our faith in Christ. If we do not get behind the shield, or we try to defend ourselves on our own, we are struck with arrows that injure us. We are choosing to place our faith in ourselves instead of falling in behind our Savior who overcame the world and Satan. We try to run, or we try to fight the arrows. But trying to protect ourselves or fight on our own can lead to self-destruction.

You make your saving help my shield, and your right hand sustains me; your help has made me great. You provide a broad path for my feet, so that my ankles do not give way. —Psalm 18:35–36

Whether through moments of faith or a long journey in which the steps alone are acts of faith in Jesus Christ, each step is worth it to bring Him glory. When you act in faith in Jesus, He protects you from fiery arrows that Satan sends your way. Getting caught by an arrow because you are running away from opportunities to stand in faith for Christ could cost you lost opportunities and, ultimately, the rewards that Christ offers for all who stand with Him.

We are children of God, and despite anything we do to disappoint Him or let him down, He will always offer us opportunities and shelter under His shield.

Questions for Reflection:

What moments of faith have you seen in your life or journey?

____

____

Where have you seen yourself in times of steadfast faith?

____

____

What are some obstacles that seem to get in your way when you take steps of faith?

____

____

Are you focusing on your battle?

____

____

What are some arrows that have hit you?

____

____

Prayer

The final part of the armor of God is prayer.

And pray in the Spirit on all occasions with all kinds of prayers and requests. With this in mind, be alert and always keep on praying for all the Lord's people. —Ephesians 6:18

Prayer comes in all forms: praise, thanksgiving, begging, pleading, or asking. Every thought, worry, or concern can be turned into a prayer. The Lord hears each word and thought you utter. He is your commander and chief, your authority, and He alone has the power to protect you! Pray on all occasions with all types of prayers.

The righteous cry out, and the Lord hears, and delivers them from all their troubles. —Psalm 34:17–18

Prayer keeps me in check, as a reminder of who is in control. As I faced close to thirty-six-plus months that ran in the same empty pattern with puffy eyes and heartbreak, there was a point when I started paying attention to Satan's tactics. I sought ways to put on the armor of God in the dark moments, and though the pain did not go away, I had confidence in what I was doing and where I was. I had peace. I was free from being trapped by emotions. I was listening to God and trying to use the time I have in the exact spot where I am to bring glory to God.

All these different parts of armor go together to protect us from the evil one; however, it is common for us to forget that God is the most important part of this armor. The armor is not ours for the choosing. When we put on the armor of God, we are not just putting on these symbols of our own ability, these symbols also give us confidence to face the battles in our everyday lives. This armor is God's armor.

"For the weapons of our warfare are not of the flesh but have divine power to destroy strongholds." 2 Corinthians 10:4

Secret Club Member: Katelyn Skillman

My Story:

I always wanted children and dreamt of one day having a family. When Miles and I got married, I told him, "When you're ready, I'm ready."

About a year into our marriage, we started trying. I felt the desire to have children was from the Lord, but I was very fearful and carried a lot of insecurity because my desire to have a child was something that I held so tightly. I even thought, *Infertility would be one of the hardest things to go through because of how strong this desire is.*

I was tracking patterns and monthly cycles. I was reading all the pregnancy materials and I just assumed I would be pregnant in the first few months. After a while, I started to get nervous, but I also knew that it had taken some people I knew six months to a year to conceive. We kept trying, but in the back of my head, I felt like something was not right. I had an intuition and I feel like it was God preparing me for what I knew in my heart.

We took the next step and went to our OB. We had labs done and everything looked good and the OB recommended that we keep trying for a full year. I remember thinking, *That is horrible but here we go.*

After we had tried for a full year, my husband got tested and the results indicated a male factor infertility. Miles carried these results as guilt and blamed himself. On one hand, I was a wife who wanted to be strong for my husband and support him through this news, and on the other, I was a woman who had desired children since a young age and was broken. Many questions filled my mind; *Will we ever be able to have our own biological children? What do we do in response to these results? What is the next step?*

Doctors gave us our options and told us that our chances to have children were very low without treatment. I was set on doing whatever it took. They told us IVF would be our only option at this point. We took it and ran! I felt as though my motivation was fear. We were going for it!

I remember some friends saying things like "Hey do you think this is going too fast, or do you feel like you are jumping into things a little quickly?" But I was unwilling to listen to anyone at that point. I was just so broken over the news that I had one focus, and that was to have a baby—whatever that meant!

Going through IVF, I had hesitations. Looking back, I wished we could have slowed down and taken our time to make decisions, but my attitude at the time was: "I'll do it. I'll do anything." I was hurt, and I was going to have a child, no matter what the cost or commitment was.

I knew that going through these tests and IVF would not guarantee a baby. I could go through the most extensive procedure for infertility, and there was the possibility we'd still be childless. The Lord kept reminding me through this process, "Yes Katelyn, that is true, but I would still be good and truthful to you no matter what."

It reminded me that my end result might not be what I dreamed of. I began to loosen the grip a little bit but continued to race hard towards the prize of holding a child.

I remember having conversations with friends and family because we wanted to feel supported and empowered as we went through IVF. We asked people what they thought about IVF. We talked about what we thought *God thought* about IVF. People even asked us hard questions like how many embryos will you store? And since we believe life starts at conception, what did we feel was appropriate about this process, and what would we do with a surplus?

We decided to have three embryos harvested, and then we

had two of them implanted. After the first round of IVF, we saw those two lines following the first transfer. Our son, Jude, grew and we had him in October. I finally felt like a first-time mom and experienced all the bliss. I remember thanking God for this baby.

Jude is a constant reminder of God's goodness to us. Then I held my hands out and gave to the Lord my ability to have children. I said, "Even if I do not have my own children biologically, you will still be faithful and good."

Then He provided a beautiful gift for us.

When Jude was around fifteen months, we started feeling the urge to have another baby. Since we had one more embryo left, we felt as though this was going to be perfect. However, God had a different plan. On the first weekend in March, I felt off and my period was late. I was really confused because we had not done the transfer for our last embryo and doctors said we could not conceive naturally, but I took a test. It was positive.

I remember the feeling of *holy cow; our bodies are not broken. God, you did this! The doctors told us we could never get pregnant, and You did this! This is amazing!*

We went to our doctor for our ten-week appointment beaming with excitement! I could not wait to hold that ultrasound image to show Jude and my family this great miracle. Having a completely healthy first pregnancy, I never even had a second thought about the possibility of negative news. But sure enough the words came from the ultrasound tech's mouth, "Measuring really small . . . need to go get a doctor."

I felt the breath taken out of me. We were left in the room alone, and Miles was trying to be positive, but I knew this was not good news. The doctor returned and said they wanted to give us a week to make sure their prediction was correct, that my body would likely miscarry.

I had no symptoms of a miscarriage, and that week was absolute torture. I spent the days on my knees begging the Lord and knowing He has the ability to sustain this life. God is a God of miracles, and I knew He could. As the week progressed, I felt crippled by the fear of the miscarriage, but on the other note, I know that God could save our miracle baby.

We returned to the imaging center a week later. They said the baby measured at the same length as the previous week, and there was no heartbeat.

From that point, I felt that closure, but waited for my body to pass our child. After rummaging through my options, we decided to have a D&C the next week. I was grateful that I did not have to miscarry at home, where it was hard to wait for my body to finally let go of our child.

I felt a little peeved. It seemed like God gave us a miracle and then took it back. The weight of mourning and grief laid on my body and soul. I spent many moments watching my son and remembering all the firsts that I would not have with this child. I knew what I was missing. I prayed that God would strengthen my weak knees because I physically felt like I could not get up some days. I knew and believed that God's ways were better and a sense of peace came over me. I remember waking up the next day with the sun shining brightly in my room and just knowing that God and His mercy was near me, by my side.

I know that people struggled to know what to say. Many knew that we had one last embryo available for another round of IVF, and so they said, "Well at least you have that baby." Yes, that was exciting. But at that moment, those words stung. I wanted the baby I lost. People do not know what to say in these situations, and I knew that they were trying to encourage me to look at the positives and to give me hope that I had the opportunity to try for our last embryo. But these words felt like false hope.

Each transfer for IVF cost $5000 and since I was only working part time, the thought of going through the process again carried a heavy financial burden. We had to question whether another transfer was doable and how we would make it work. After our miscarriage, our desire to have a baby was multiplied by a thousand. I was ready to put in the deposit. This is what I wanted and hoped for.

Five months later we transferred our last embryo. Ten days after the transfer, they did a blood test to find out if I was pregnant. I remember waiting those ten days and telling Miles, "I do not know if I am pregnant, I just do not know if this is it."

He was always so supportive and encouraging and would remind me of the hope that we needed to have with each step moving forward. I was waiting for a phone call telling us of my results. On the day that they called, we were driving home from the zoo and the woman on the phone said, "I am sorry, but unfortunately you are not pregnant."

I was in shock again. We drove home in silence, and I could feel sadness and anger building. I can remember questions arising like, "What? Why is this happening? I just lost a baby five months ago. How could this not work?"

I felt like God owed me this gift. I felt all the loss piling up on itself and felt the grief of losing two babies in six months. An embryo was a life to us and we felt the weight of losing our child.

From that point, I decided I was done with medical intervention. I still wanted more children, and I knew that I was meant to be a mom of multiple kids. So, my question turned to, "God, would you continue to show us our next steps."

I prayed for the next several months about what the Lord wanted for us. My personality was always to be a go-getter and if I did not have something that I wanted; I was going to go after it. These months spent in prayer, were a time for me to step back, process the grief, and figure out what would come next.

We started being open to adoption in any form, domestically or internationally. Meanwhile I knew other people who were struggling to get pregnant with their first, and I felt guilty. My previous self would have said, "Do not complain, and do not be sad, because you already have a child." I wrestled with guilt for wanting another child.

Time passed and I heard about someone going through embryo adoption. Even though I was familiar with the IVF process, embryo adoption was foreign to me. This is a process of adopting someone's unused embryos. People donated their extra embryos to other families to have children. The embryos carry their own DNA and are frozen awaiting a transfer.

God had shown me through my own IVF journey with Jude, the beauty and value of life as an embryo. I became passionate about this opportunity. My heart broke for the number of lives that were waiting in a freezer to be adopted. So many couples out there hold the weight of having all these embryos, and they do not know what to do with them. On the other hand, other women desire to carry a child and give birth to a baby.

I was not sure if this was an option for us but I knew that God had laid this on my heart to advocate for. Questions started to surface when we began looking into this option for ourselves. I was nervous about going through another failed transfer or possibly another miscarriage. I weighed the options of infant adoption. I knew that would also be messy and hard, but I was guaranteed a baby at the end. It would take a long time, but I would not experience loss. I was scared and unsure what to do.

Something kept drawing us back to embryo adoption. Miles stepped up in our time of wavering decisions and told me that embryo adoption was where his heart was, and what he thought should be the next step for our family. I was going to trust that his guidance was from the Lord, and we were going to do this.

We looked into embryo adoption agencies. I learned as much as I could by reading stories and trying to soak up information. Embryo adoption is much like traditional adoption with tons of paperwork, applications, and home studies but I found Facebook support groups, success stories, and I even met Ellen, who was in the process of embryo adoption. Finally, we were at the point with the agency of waiting to be matched. We gave our waiting to the Lord and knew that no matter what nationality, race, or number of embryos, we were open to the Lord's plan.

In one of the Facebook groups that I was in, a woman posted that she was thinking about donating her embryos. She was Chinese, and she and her husband had moved from China ten years earlier. She was looking for someone to adopt her five embryos.

I immediately screenshotted the post and sent it to Miles. I felt a strong pull to reach out to this woman. At this point we had already invested in an agency and had spent about $3000, but we decided to message her anyway. Once we started talking with her, we never stopped. We were very open about being Christians. We talked about good questions, hard questions, race questions, plans for raising these children and what it would look like. She wanted her children to go to a family that understood and valued these lives. Our conversation continued and she finally said, "I think we are a match." We walked away from our adoption agency and adopted this woman's five embryos.

We had started talking in March, and by July we had the five embryos at our doctor's office. I wanted to make sure that I gave these babies the best opportunity for survival as possible so I started eating better and exercising. From March till our transfer, I lost about thirty pounds. I had not been aware of the unhealthy relationship I had built with food after the losses. Changing my habits helped me process through the emotions and grief instead of hiding behind them. God gave me joy in the change and exercise to help encourage me in the next steps.

When we transferred in July, I felt confident in my body emotionally, spiritually and physically but more importantly, I knew God had led us here, and if His plan was to give us life, it would be in His hands. Our five embryos had been in a freezer for six years and we were excited to try for them. We planned to transfer two embryos, which had been frozen in the same straw. As we walked out of the office, I felt like we were really going to have twins and both embryos would survive.

I continued holding my breath, and I battled the fears and questions that come in the waiting time, but we had an odd sense of peace. Ten days went by and we found out we were expecting twins. A few months later, we found out that they were both boys. This matched an encounter that we had with a gentleman before our years of trying. A random man had said he had a word from the Lord and proceeded to pray for twin boys that I would carry and have. This is one of those moments that looking back seemed crazy at the time but was beyond our understanding. God uses ordinary people to give hope.

I would have never imagined my family in this way, but this was not our doing. It was God's! We are thankful that we kept walking, and had open arms to what God wanted. The journey was hard, and I will always walk with a limp because of our steps but it reminds me of all places where we have been and the obstacles we have overcome.

Did any scriptures/songs/stories stick with you during your journey?

• Psalm 69:13: *But as for me, my prayer is to you, O Lord. At an acceptable time, O God, in the abundance of your steadfast love answer me in your saving faithfulness.*

• Hebrews 12:12–13: *Therefore lift your drooping hands and strengthen your weak knees, and make straight paths for your feet, so that what is lame may not be put out of joint but rather be healed.*

"Who You Say I Am" - Hillsong United. It reminded me that I do not need to be a slave to fear.

Do you do anything to remember the lives you lost?

We do an outing together and just celebrate life together.

What would you say to women who are going through something similar to your experience?

Cling to hope and cling to who God says He is. Cling to what His promises to you. He does not say that He will promise a baby through this, but He is greater than anything. He will satisfy you. But be open to His plans and live life open armed. He is faithful to meet us in our dark places and He can handle our ups and our downs. He remains steadfast and sovereign. It is OK to ask questions and search for God. He knows your emotions, and He can handle it.

Our Children:

Jude – 4 years old; Addis – 1 year old; Abe – 1 year old; Baby Skillman #2 – Due date 11/11/2017; Baby Skillman #3 – Due date 6/8/2018.

Chapter 3 - The Right Solution

I hate those who pay regard in worthless idols but I trust in the Lord I will rejoice and be glad in your steadfast love, because you have seen my affliction; because you have known the distress of my soul, and you have not delivered me into the hands of the enemy; you have set my feet in a broad place. —Psalm 31:6–8

There was a time in my life when I would pray to not be pregnant. I spent my first few years of college running rampant in sin and enjoying all the pleasures that this world had to offer. I knew what I was doing was wrong but I did not care. I claimed to be a follower of Jesus Christ, and my attitude was such a shallow understanding of redemption. I figured that He would just forgive me later. Ironically, the gift I was so careless with was my hardest battle that I have ever had to face.

It is hard to tell in this life what is a punishment, discipline, a consequence, or what is just pain and suffering that is brought by this sinful world. So many times I saw the verse from Psalm 127:3, *"Children are a heritage from the Lord, offspring a reward from Him."* This verse would crawl under my skin. I could feel the jealousy of women who were given children. *Why was I not able to conceive? God why do I not receive a reward? Am I not good enough? Did I make too many mistakes?* I would sink back into the moments of darkness that were part of my previous years, wishing I could make a different choice because now I did not deserve the gift of a child. I started to chain myself back to the sin of this world.

If you truly claim Christ as your Savior and believe that he died on the cross for all your sins; yesterday, today, and in the future, then you know you are forgiven. You can hold your head high and not sink back to worrying about what could have been if only you had made different choices. Christ paid the price and already freed you from those chains.

• *"I, I am He who blots out your transgressions for my own sake, and I will not remember your sins" (Isaiah 43:25).*

• *"As far as the east is from the west, so far He removes our transgressions for us" (Psalm 103:2).*

• *"He does not deal with us according to our sin nor repay us according to our iniquities" (Psalm 103:10).*

• *"Brothers, I do not consider that I have made it my own. But one thing I do: forgetting what lies behind and straining forward to what lies ahead. I press toward the goal for the prize of the upward call of God in Christ Jesus" (Philippians 3:13–14).*

God has given you those desires in your heart for a reason. He has you exactly where He wants you. What now? What do we do with this desire and no direction? How do we know what is right?

Do not take this task lightly. If you ask, you must be willing to listen and the more challenging part is that you must be willing to follow His direction. Are you willing to ask, listen, and follow?

When I ask questions with closed answers like *Lord, may I please be blessed with a child?* I may receive an answer, but I also could receive silence. Am I willing to accept an answer that is not a yes? or what if the answer is "Yes, but not right now." When we limit our vision to only accepting an answer to one specific want, we close our minds to the possibility that God may want to use that desire in a different way.

God is a patient God and will wait until our heart, spirit, and mind are ready and open to His plan. When we come with open arms, we allow God to show up in ways that we never could have dreamed, and we are moving towards the goal and calling of Christ Jesus instead of the American dream. My questions changed to what do you want for me? How do you want us to proceed? You gave me this desire Lord, and I want to use it to honor you, show me my next step.

Once we ask, we have to wait and listen. You have the Holy Spirit inside of you who will guide you to the answers through the Bible. The Spirit will use surroundings to also encourage and confirm the answer. Things will line up. You will experience a peace, maybe a song, have a unique conversation that you cannot explain, a continuous thought that seems foreign but is always present. However, all answers that you receive will always align with scripture. Scripture is the sword of the spirit and will give wisdom in every situation with the molding of your spirit. However, I want to throw a warning flag. Satan loves to distract and confuse you from making a decision that lines up with to God's plan. He will pull your focus elsewhere.

"But each person is tempted when he is lured and enticed by his own desire." James 1:14

Satan will try to tempt you with a route that *appears* easier or shorter but that is not the truth of God. The Holy Spirit will not abandon you in these times—you could feel uneasiness, anxiety, the feeling that something is not right. All these can be guiding measures used to steer you to the right path. If you are struggling with hearing God's answer, bring it back to the Lord. Pray for discernment and guidance. God will not abandon you. He wants His children to seek Him and His will.

"But if from there you seek the Lord your God, you will find him if

you seek him with all your heart and with all your soul" Deuteronomy 4:29

Sometimes the answers God gives seem vague, while at other times, they are specific. Once you have discerned your answer and know what the Lord wants for you, you are given a step of obedience to take. Failing to obey can result in discipline, consequences, and missed opportunities for you and others. Not following the Lord's instructions is disobedience.

And Samuel said, "What is more pleasing to the Lord: your burnt offerings and sacrifices or your obedience to his voice? Listen! Obedience is better than sacrifice, and submission is better than offering the fat of rams. Rebellion is as sinful as witchcraft and stubbornness as bad as worshiping idols. So because you have rejected the command of the Lord, he has rejected you as king. —1 Samuel 15:22–23

Disobedience is a hard word to wrap our head around, and sometimes I even justify my disobedience so that I feel better about myself. God does not tolerate disobedience. But even in my disobedience, God has a steadfast and pursuing love for me. There are times I experience discipline because God is a loving father and discipline molds our spirit into the person He will use to bring him glory.

God has seen your pain and heard your cries; He wants to use these times to glorify his name. He wants us to look back and say, "I can see the Lord's hand in this." The Lord wants us to continue to mold your spirit to look more and more like Him. He will take your feet on this narrow road and place them confidently on His path for you.

I battled every day to wake up, be obedient, and not get distracted by or focused on what worked for other people. Instead I worked to keep my eyes on what the Lord wanted me to do right then, where I was, and to accept His plan and not my own.

One of the more common stories in the Bible about infertility is Abraham and Sarah. Despite Abraham, being ninety-nine, God gave the couple a baby boy. This story is so much more than them waiting and receiving a child. It shows the struggles and hardships that both Abraham and Sarah had to go through. It shows the perseverance, mistakes and healing that the Lord brought them. Their story is long but is a great passage of scripture found in Genesis 12–23.

Abraham, originally known as Abram was a wealthy, well known man who was called to faith by the Lord. The Lord spoke several times directly to Abram and the first time He said,

"Go from your country, and your kindred and your father's house to the land that I will show you. And I will make of you a great nation, and I will bless you and make your name great, so that you will be a blessing. I will bless those who bless you, and him who dishonors you I will curse, and in you all the families of the earth shall be blessed." (Genesis 12:1–3)

The Lord had promised to make Abram a great nation with many descendants and give his family land. Abram knew that in time the land would be given to him, but the idea of descendants seemed to cause confusion for Abram. At the time Abram left his homeland, he was seventy-five years old and his wife Sarai, later known as Sarah, was sixty-five, which was well past the child bearing years. The Bible made it clear that to this point, Sarai was unable to bear children. Yet, throughout the years, God's words were faithful, and He repeated to himself multiple times that the descendants would be of Abram:

"They would be as the dust of the earth, so that if one can count the

dust of the earth, your offspring can also be counted" (Genesis 13:16).

At the time, if a man died and had no children, his possessions would be left to the heir of the house, which was the eldest child of a servant who was born in the household. Years went by, and Abram and Sarai were still childless. Abram started to question whether God would grant them a child through their own bodies or whether it was a figure of speech and his possessions would pass to the heir of the house. God answered and renewed his promise to Abram.

"'This man shall not be your heir; your very own son shall be your heir.' And He brought him outside and said, 'Look toward heaven, and number the stars, if you are able to number them.' Then He said to him, 'So shall your offspring be.' And he [Abram] believed the Lord, and he [Lord] counted it to him as righteousness" (Genesis 15:4–6).

Abram believed and waited on the Lord. So often, as Christ followers, we are called to wait. Satan uses our flesh to create tension and make us want to act instead of waiting. So many times, we let our armor down and are filled with doubt. We act out in the desires and callings of our flesh, which distracts us from the Lord's will.

In 2018, I was sick of waiting. This year was going to be different. It was time for me to check and see if there was anything I could do for myself. As January came about, I decided to get a few tests done to make sure everything was still good to go since this was going to be the year we would become a party of three. I convinced myself nothing was wrong with making that appointment with my regular doctor and getting a blood panel done again. Shocker . . . Everything came back at normal levels. I heard the words once again that I was used to: "Nothing is *wrong*."

That would be music to most people's ears but I felt like if I could have something wrong, at least I could place blame on having to wait on something that I could see and understand. That was, of course, selfish of me, and my flesh was lashing out at anything it could grasp onto for hope.

My doctor offered to send a referral to a reproductive specialist. An eerie feeling came over me but I agreed to the referral and went on my way.

As I walked to the car from my doctor's office, I envisioned walking on this narrow path of obedience and starting to feel the shoulder bumps on the side. It seemed as though the width of my path was more confining with each step I took. I could feel the tension of spiritual warfare at hand.

What was I doing? The Lord was so clear to me *"just wait, my timing is made perfect, just wait."* Instead of recognizing the emotions and underlying battle that I was experiencing, I pursued the tension. I wanted to look for a way to do what the Lord instructed and still get what I wanted. I looked for any angle that I could use to convince myself that going to a reproductive specialist was "obedient" in the Lord's eyes. My questioning and pursuit of this alternate way to walk my path opened an opportunity for this world, my flesh, and Satan to take hold of me and tempt me in ways that I was not prepared for.

Quickly, I began sinking back into my flesh and finding a way into my emotions through feelings of doubt. I felt doubt that God would ever answer my prayer, feelings that His answer of *"wait"* actually meant never. Maybe God just needed me to give my body a little nudge in the right direction and actually wanted me to go to the specialist. I mean so many other people are given direction from God to do IVF, hormone therapy, trigger shots, prescriptions, etc. These people had babies through the help and assistance of modern-day medicine. I wanted that too. I wanted options. I wanted answers. I wanted those answers, I wanted a child. I did not want to wait.

That afternoon I made a phone call to the Kansas City Reproductive Specialist and set up an appointment for March.

"Now Sarai, Abram's wife, had borne him no children. She had a female Eygptian servant whose name was Hagar. And Sarai said to Abram, 'Behold now, the Lord has prevented me from bearing children. Go in my servant; it may be that I shall obtain children by her.' And Abram listened to the voice of Sarai" (Genesis 16:2).

Sarai decided to take matters into her own hands, and instead of seeking the Lord, created a plan to get a descendant through another woman. Hagar was Egyptian. Egyptians were shown in the Bible as a people who followed their flesh, pleasures and worshipped many gods. Hagar was a servant given to Abram and Sarai when they fled to Egypt. Sarai gave Hagar to Abram as a concubine. If Hagar had any children, Sarai would have full and legal rights to any children as descendants.

This situation and solution were not the Lord's direction. These were not the steps the Lord was asking Abram and Sarai to take. In the Bible every detail is not presented, but I do believe that scripture is not missing anything and each word is ordained and spoken by God. These chapters show an absence of Sarai seeking the Lord's understanding in her path; in fact it shows that Sarai was listening to her own voice and flesh when she made these decisions to create a solution to her "*problem*" of waiting.

Abram, who was given direct instructions from the Lord that said his offspring would be his own son, listened to his wife's voice as well, instead of seeking the direct instructions from God. This passage so clearly shows that when a husband and a wife are not seeking the Lord for understanding, they are easily distracted by their own voices and answers that show up in this world. Why did Sarai not ask God how or why? Why did she not ask the Lord if she should give Hagar to her husband to get a son?

Nowhere in the Bible does it say that she sought the Lord after devising this solution.

Have you ever wanted to ask the Lord if something or some circumstance was where you were supposed to be, but you refused to ask the question? There was a hesitation, not because asking was hard, but because you were scared of the answer that you may receive.

This hesitation should be a red flag. This should have been a red flag to me, Sarai, and anyone else who is unwilling to ask the question of how, why, or what do you want me to do, Lord? If I am unwilling to listen and respond in the way that the Lord wants me to, I am being driven by my flesh, because I am scared to face the Lord's answer.

The flesh and the spirit always want opposite things. One seeks glory for God while the other seeks glory and fulfillment for one's self. We need to ask and seek when every opportunity arises, not just assume that everything is an opened door by God. The Lord will make it clear when waiting is done if you are seeking Him.

Waiting is always longer than we think it should be. We will always be driven to act before the waiting is done. Are you willing to wait if He calls you to? Are you willing to ask and seek His solutions and not your own? If you are too scared to hand over control to God, He will either continue to wait and be patient, or He will get your attention. Regardless, His plan will show through, whether you are willing or not.

Setting up a meeting with a reproductive specialist is no quick thing. I made an appointment for several weeks out and was anticipating the appointment. I hoped my eyes would be opened to all these options that were available. I had a few people that I felt comfortable talking with a few people about my true feelings, but every time I told others what I wanted to do, got an uneasy feeling in my stomach. As soon as the words came that I had made an appointment, I felt the need to justify myself and explain why I was taking these steps. The person I was talking with would go along with it, empowering me and telling me about someone else who also went down that path. I would pause and ask myself who I was really trying to convince. Was it this person or was I trying to convince God?

As I walked into the specialist doctor's office, I had convinced myself that this step was not anything against the Lord, but if I stopped talking to myself, I could feel the conviction creep up. So, I kept talking to myself. I waited in that office, watched the videos on genetic testing, signed, and filled out all the forms about my history and medical needs, and what I desired in this visit. I was led into a conference room, and a nurse came in with the news that there were no "red flags" in my medical history and proceeded to tell me about the endless options that we could embark on to start our family. They wanted to do one final blood draw, and then they would wait to do the first procedure during a specific time in my cycle.

Walking back to the car, I felt my flesh encouraged but my spirit felt like a dog with its tail between its legs. Shouldn't I have been happy? Wasn't this what I wanted, options?

And he [Abram] went into Hagar, and she conceived. And when she saw that she had conceived, she looked with contempt on her mistress. And Sarai said to Abram, "May the wrong done to me be on you! I gave my servant to your embrace, and when she saw that she had conceived, she looked on me with contempt. May the Lord judge between you and me!" But Abram said to Sarai, "Behold your servant is in your power; do to her as you please." Then Sarai dealt harshly with her and she fled from her. —Genesis 16:4–6

Sometimes God gives us the very thing we are chasing after despite His guidance. Even in the beautiful gifts that our own solutions can produce, the Lord's guidance and discipline will show through. After Hagar became pregnant, just as Sarai wanted, Sarai's jealousy built and she probably knew that she was truly the barren one because Abram could clearly produce a child. She did not claim the child as her own; instead, she blamed Abram for not guiding her appropriately. Abram put it back on Sarai by allowing her freedom to treat Hagar poorly.

Christ followers are set apart by their decision-making. People of this world are driven by their desires, goals, careers, and feelings but Christ followers make decisions based on guidance from the Lord. When Abram and Sarai did not seek guidance from the Lord, they were left with their own solutions. Neither of them was asking the Lord if having intercourse with Hagar was what Abram should be doing. Instead, they both went down the path to use the sin of multiple wives to accomplish the promise given to Abram by God.

Very quickly, they realized the path was not right, and neither one wanted to take responsibility for their solution. The repercussions from this solution broke a relationship between Sarai and Hagar. Instead of Sarai being an example of a woman of faith, Sarai showed hatred towards Hagar.

I spent the drive home from the specialist thinking. I was fighting the convicting feelings of the Holy Spirit that were trying to guide me against going through with any of the options with the specialist. What if we just did some tests to be able to *know*? What harm could that do? If the results came in with something simple, then at least we could weigh a solution.

I started to envision the feelings and emotions of receiving news of our results and a pressuring question came from within me. Would it *actually* be better to know? I envisioned my husband, my best friend, the leader of our family being told that he had a male infertility factor and that it was probably causing our struggles with infertility. I could almost feel the burden and blame that he would fight as the weight was lowered onto his shoulders.

Even if he put on a good face for me, I could already see the discouragement that would always be under the surface. I could hear my responses and conversations that I would use trying to lift that weight off of him. Then the situation flipped; what if Kyle was completely healthy, and I was the one who had something wrong? What guilt and heartache would I feel about this body that I had? I could feel everything just screaming that *I am not enough*. Would it create distance between Kyle and me? Would it create tension? Blame? And for what . . . to get knowledge? What would knowledge really accomplish in this situation? I would be opening the door for distance in our marriage and personal struggles that would chain me to this world once again.

God was trying to protect me. He gave me a command to wait. When I started to entertain the idea of pursuing other options, He opened my eyes to the goodness of His protection. God was protecting my relationship with Kyle and with myself. When Kyle and I got married, we tied a knot but our commitment was not just with Kyle and me, but also with God.

Our decisions have to be tethered to God's will. We have to seek Him for our decisions, and if we do not, we can persuade ourselves into solutions that will not change the outcome but can damage relationships we already have.

Kyle and I discussed it and decided that we would wait to proceed until we were out of debt. I did not have the nerve to just say, *"I do not feel right about this"* or *"this is not what God wants me to do."*

I know medical intervention is the answer God gives so many other women, but it was not the one He gave me. I continued to take a vitamin or two, secretly hoping I could get pregnant and go, "AHA, that's what the problem was." I wanted to blame something, because just saying God does not think it is the right time is impossible to understand. However, nothing, every month resulted in another single lined test, a broken heart, roller coaster of emotions, and turning my focus on my empty arms.

Hagar gave birth to a son for Abram and named him, Ishmael. Even though Hagar returned, there was strife between Sarah and Hagar. Thirteen years go by and the Lord communicated again to Abram:

And God said to Abraham, "As for Sarai your wife, you shall not call her Sarai but Sarah shall be her name. I will bless her, and moreover, I will give you a son by her. I will bless her, and she shall become nations; kings of peoples shall come from her." Then Abraham fell on his face and laughed and said to himself, "Shall a child be born to a man who is a hundred years old? Shall Sarah, who is ninety years old, bear a child?"

And Abraham said to God, "Oh that Ishmael might live before you!" God said, "No but your wife shall bear a son, and you shall call his name Isaac. I will establish my covenant with him as an everlasting covenant for his offspring after him. As for Ishmael, I have heard you; behold, I have blessed him and will make him fruitful and multiply him greatly. He shall father twelve princes, and I will make him a great nation. But I will establish my covenant with Isaac, whom Sarah shall bear to you at this time next year" (Genesis 17:16–21).

Sarah was probably to the point in her life where she was no longer able to bear children, referred commonly today as menopause. There is no way humanly possible that she could conceive a child. Abraham even questioned God, *"Oh you mean through my son Ishmael.* God blatantly said no. He had a plan from the beginning to bless Sarah and Abraham with a child. Even though they tried to come up with a solution to fulfill God's plan, God was not going to use their solution. They tried to help God, but God did not need help for His sovereign will. Their desire to try to have a child at the time they wanted it clouded and distracted them from the path that God had intended for them.

After reading this, I felt convicted and a little frustrated. Why would God not come right out and tell me whether I would have a child or not? If He did, it would be so much easier to wake up each day and not be bogged down by the desire to have a child. If He did, I could wait and have confidence that my time would come. When you read back through this story, you see that God promised a child to Abraham and Sarah almost twenty-five years before they were given one. Do you think that made the waiting easy? Do you think knowing that one day they would hold a child in their arms was comforting? or did it open up opportunities to doubt God? Obviously, we see that it was not easy for Hagar, and they were not perfect.

What about when Sarah went through menopause and then was still promised a child despite the understanding that there was no humanly possible way for her to conceive?

Nothing is easy. Whether we are given a detailed answer or a vague answer from God, there is always room for doubt. As beautiful as it seems for God to directly talk to Abraham and give such detail of a plan, God only communicated with him about four times over the twenty-five years. Imagine the times of waiting.

What Abraham would have given to have direction and counsel from God every day! We have that. We have the Bible, which contains God's words to guide us as we question and seek to understand what our answers from God mean. We are given comfort, encouragement, criticism, and hope. Hope not in the answer that we are waiting on, but hope in Jesus Christ and His plan for our future on this earth and in eternity.

The Lord visited Sarah as he had said, and the Lord did to Sarah as He had promised. And Sarah conceived and bore Abraham a son in his old age at the time of which God had spoken to him. Abraham called the name of his son who was born to him, whom Sarah bore him, Isaac. —

Genesis 21:1–3

God is big. God is bigger and more powerful than anything in this world. No medicine, no procedure, no human nature, nothing can stand in His way. We cannot help Him and we cannot stop Him. God follows through on His word every single time.

Have you asked Him the question you have been trying to solve yourself? Have you asked if you are on the right path? Every woman's path is different. Every answer from God is different, so how do we know if we are making a right decision? Infertility is not a new problem. Women all the way back to the beginning have struggled to understand family planning, and each one has received different answers from God.

Abram and Sarai - Promised a child but had to wait over twenty-five years (Genesis 12–23).

Manoah and wife - Wife was barren and an angel told her she would have a child. She conceived and had Samson (Judges 13).

Isaac and Rebekah - Rebekah was barren. Isaac asked the Lord for a child and He blessed them with twins, Esau and Jacob (Genesis 25).

Jacob and Rachel - God opened Rachel's womb and they had Joseph and Benjamin (Genesis 29–30).

Hannah and Elkanah - Hannah wept for a son and she had Samuel and 5 additional children. Samuel went to serve in the Lord's house (1 Samuel 1).

Elisabeth and Zachariah - Both were barren and an angel appeared and promised a son and they had John the Baptist (Luke 1).

All of these couples were barren; all of them received different answers from God. They asked, listened, and followed the Lord's directions. None of these people were perfect. They expressed hesitations or doubts or were caught in distractions, but God was faithful and fulfilled His promise. God blessed each couple with a child, and for some there were many. Each child was given at an exact time and in an exact way that was instrumental in the gospel. God had a 100 percent success rate for infertility issues in the Bible, and He has an answer for you. Come to Him with open arms and remember that He is the same God who gave Sarah a child after menopause, answered the weeping women, and gave children to the barren, He did it all for His glory and not a moment too soon.

In the early summer of 2018, I finally came to the point that I was ready to not only listen to God's answer of "wait," but to also be open to how God wanted to use me exactly where I was. I looked for ways to talk about Kyle's and my journey. I wanted to learn how to love on people who evoked my envy due to their having children or a family. I started to become aware of weaknesses in my battle against evil thoughts and Satan's tactics and started to fight back as I obeyed God's answer to wait.

I had many successful days and many hard days, but I was dedicated to spending every day to make the most for Jesus Christ. I had strange peace with the unknowingness of God's plan and knew that God would sustain me even if I never held a child in my arms. His grace was enough for me, and I would give up on grasping after my wants for this world. I knew this was true for me when I lost my obsession with checking early pregnancy symptoms and when my expected monthly visitor started seeming unexpected.

One normal Sunday morning in September, I had a weird thought. I immediately pulled out my phone to check my calendar. I was past the expected timing for my period. Like usual, I was running late to church, and now I needed to stop to buy a pregnancy test. I got ready, jumped in the car, ran into the store and then sped to church.

I opened the box and slid the pink-wrapped test into my coat pocket. As I rushed to the bathroom at the church and pulled the test out of my coat pocket, I felt numb. *I do not want to do the emotional roller coaster again.* So I kept myself calm to await the expected negative result. I looked down at that test to see two pink lines.

Questions for Reflection:

What part of your journey or trial do you struggle with wanting to fix yourself?

____

____

Is there a part of your journey that you feel eerie or uneasy about?

____

____

In what ways do you see God's grace in your situation?

____

____

Secret Club Member: Melanie Davidson

My Story:

My husband and I wanted to start a family from the moment we got married. We love kids and could not wait to have our own! We tried mostly on our own for about three years, and then sought a natural doctor's advice. We did some testing, I started taking a few supplements, and I did all the charting, temperature taking, and tracking of fertility signs. It was a lot!

I became overwhelmed by all of the "stuff" I had to do very diligently. So we decided to stop. That very night, I felt absolute peace like I had never felt before. It took about another year of trying to conceive on our own. We found out on March 8, 2020 that we were expecting our sweet baby girl, Gracelyn!

That's just the physical side. The rest of the four-and-a-half years of trying were much more complicated emotionally and spiritually. We experienced many tears, stressful times in our marriage, and lessons learned along the way. People lifted us up, encouraged us, and made our burden lighter. And others, even with the best of intentions, fed us false hope and tried to convince us that if we only did this or that, it would just happen—like it was magic or something. But we had so much more to learn during those years of waiting. There was a perfect time for it to happen. And only God knew just how it would all unfold.

When you were waiting for a child, what did you find most challenging?

Not knowing what to do. Most of the time, I never felt the Lord leading us to do any specific thing. So it was difficult to determine if we should seek medical intervention or not. We did try a few supplements, a cleanse, and some blood tests for about a year after we'd been trying for three years and hadn't conceived yet. I remember being so overwhelmed by everything I had to do, supplements to take, and things I had to track that we decided to just stop all of it. The night we decided that, I felt absolute peace like I had never felt about it ever before.

Was there a scripture/song/Bible story that stuck with you throughout your journey?

I waited patiently for the Lord; And He inclined to me, and heard my cry. He also brought me up out of a horrible pit, out of the miry clay, and set my feet upon a rock, and established my steps. He has put a new song in my mouth— Praise to our God; Many will see it and fear, and will trust in the Lord. -- Psalm 40:1–3:

Portions of this psalm spoke to me at different times in our journey.

Verse 1: Often Satan made me feel like verse 1 was untrue, that just because God hadn't answered the way I wanted Him to, He hadn't heard my cry.

Verse 2: Feelings came in waves. At times, I felt all right about the situation, and at other times I'd feel as though I were stuck in this devastating pit. Verse 3: Around the same time that we decided to quit all the interventions, the Lord spoke so clearly to me: Infertility (or any other trial) doesn't have to be a devastating experience. It can be as joyful and faith-building as you want it to be. It did *not* define me. He put a new song in my mouth because He enlightened my heart to understand the purpose of this difficulty in my life: to make Him known.

The purpose of my life was not to receive pity from others or have an excuse for being sad because of my circumstances. God taught me how to be defined by Him alone, and that in turn, others will come to know Him (whether for the first time or just be encouraged again) through my joyful witness even during a difficult trial.

As I meditated on each piece of these verses, God's power would overwhelm my sorrow if I would let it, and I had such intimate times with Him! Oh, I would cry tears of joy at times. But it took me fully turning my heart to Him, and nothing else, to find contentment in my circumstance.

Forever Reign by Hillsong Worship. I felt empty, like something was missing at times, but nothing could ultimately fill me up but Him!

What would you say to a woman who was going through something similar to what you experienced?

Keep a journal! I didn't do this until we were about three years into our infertility journey, but it made all the difference! I would write things in it that God would speak to me, songs that touched my heart, and scripture that moved me.

I'd read through that journal as often as I could, multiple times on the hard days. I would cry and pray over the truths in it, and I could honestly feel God change my sorrow and anger into joy and delight!

One incredible blessing that infertility brought to my life was the fellowship with friends who were walking through the same trial. There's nothing like being able to talk to a friend who knows exactly what you're going through! Having said that, you have the freedom to share your struggles with whomever you want to, but be careful what advice you take to heart. Make sure it's biblical. Banking on false hope and shallow claims will only leave you feeling emptier. So seek people who will truly point you to the Lord.

One day I was having a really difficult time because that "time of the month" had come again. I confided in a godly friend who didn't know about this aspect of my life yet and she gave me some of the best advice: Don't look inward at yourself; look up! Fix your eyes on Jesus.

Learn to be content with what you have and where you are in your life right now. You have the choice to be just as discontent with the circumstances that come your way with or without a child. Hold fast to what you know about God, not what you feel. Abide in Him!

Chapter 4 - Why Is This Happening?

"Be gracious to me, O Lord, for I am in distress; my eye is wasted from grief; my soul and my body also. For my life is spent with sorrow, and my years with sighing; my strength fails because of my iniquity, and my bones waste away." — Psalm 31:9–10

I did not even recognize the indication that I was pregnant when I first saw it. I was just taking a test quickly before heading into the church service. Staring at the test, I started taking deep slow breaths to take in this moment that I had waited years to see. I started mentally preparing myself for the fact that I would have to hold this secret in for almost an hour and half before telling Kyle.

Ok Brianna, Kyle has to be the first one to know. Do not blow this Brianna! Keep it together for just one hour, and then you can tell Kyle.

Kyle was working lights in the back of the church, and I was sitting with my sister for the service. I remember having to squish through the row to my seat since everyone was already worshiping. It was during late September so I had tucked the test in the inside pocket of my jacket. Of course, with my luck, as soon as I got to my seat, I realized my inside pocket of my jacket had a hole in it and the test slipped onto the floor.

I quickly bent and made it seem like I was putting my stuff under the seat. Fortunately, my sister did not see it or think twice about my sporadic movements that made me bump into her and everyone around us. I finally started worshiping, and I could not keep in the tears. I was worshipping and thanking God with all I had.

I could hardly even believe what I had seen earlier. My sister did not think too much about my crying since I am an emotional person. I cry quite frequently, so after 25 years of knowing me, this did not flag her attention at all.

Throughout the service, I could hardly focus. I was counting down the seconds until I could tell Kyle. I started thinking of creative ways to tell him, but I realized that it was just silly. I would not be able to keep it a secret anyway.

Once we were dismissed, I waited until the lighting/tech booth was clear, said goodbye to my sister, and rushed up to Kyle. I could not wait. I just blurted it out: *Guess what . . . I am pregnant*!

He threw his arms around me and we went out to the car. Since my family is part of our church community, we tried to avoid conversation with anyone because it would be next to impossible for me to keep a secret this good.

Later that week, we told our families. Everyone was over the moon. Yet, through the excitement, I had an eerie feeling. I was worried, and I was nervous for the next few weeks. I knew the family history of pregnancy loss that I held. I was afraid to get attached to my child and then lose it. We told our families early because we wanted them to share in the excitement that we had all waited for and also so they could pray for the next few weeks.

I was proactive in my pregnancy, I went to the doctor, asked all the right questions, and found the perfect doctor to deliver my child. I wanted a doctor who took my information and helped me make good decisions and cared about my medical family history with pregnancies. She immediately had blood work done to check all my levels and recommended an ultrasound to pin down the due date.

At six weeks we had the most beautiful moment in the women's imaging center. We got to see our little one and hear that quick light heartbeat. Hearing tiny thuds made it so real for me. It was an absolute miracle. To say we were excited was an understatement. We were oozing with joy. It felt so real, and awakening to the reality of having a child was amazing! God had finally answered us with a "Yes." Our waiting was done. Our family was a party of three.

A few weeks went by. Morning sickness was at its finest, which resulted in my being confused about what to eat, how to work out, how to bend, sleep, all of it. Despite all the illness, I was not upset; I was loving every second of being pregnant! I had found every app about the size that my child was at that stage and read all the crazy facts and information about the development of our little bean.

Three weeks had passed since my last ultrasound. I was now just over nine weeks when I saw on Facebook an ad for women between eight to twelve weeks of pregnancy to come and be models for training ultrasound techs at women's clinic in town. This clinic operates to encourage young women who are pregnant to think about options besides abortions.

I loved this clinic and immediately signed up! I could not wait to see our little cherry-sized baby! I made the appointment and was scheduled to go later that week.

The morning of the ultrasound, I was still sick as ever, but it was worth every second. I prepped and drank as instructed. I remember going in and getting all the checks and practically running to the bed to get the gel put on my belly. They walked me through what they were going to do. Several ultrasound techs were in the room, and they all took turns running through the equipment and prep procedures. Kyle came by and joined to get a glimpse of our baby. As we looked at the giant TV, I could not quite make out any specific body parts, but I had no doubt that the ultrasound techs knew what they were doing. I looked back over at the doctor, and I realized the techs had left, and he was now the only one in the room with Kyle and me. He shut off the machine and to this day, I have no idea exactly what he said. The words that held on to me were, *"No heartbeat . . . very small . . . Go to your doctor as soon as possible."*

And just like that, all excitement was gone. My heart dropped to my stomach. I was still; I could not even feel my own heartbeat. My body was in shock. It felt as if everything moved to slow motion.

The doctor left and I looked up at Kyle, who immediately came over and hugged me. He started to cry. I, of course, hugged him back, but I could not even believe what was happening. I could not cry, or process the words I had heard.

They checked us out of the clinic and the nurse prayed for us. I was in such a daze; I do not remember even closing my mouth after the news. I was just struck with unbelief.

I remember so vividly coming home from the ultrasound specialist and just falling on the floor weeping, face to the ground, begging the Lord for the news we heard to not be true. We had waited for this child for three years, and God had finally said yes. All the questions started to swarm to me . . . Why had God changed His mind? Why would He do this? Why would He even allow us to get pregnant if He was just going to take our baby away? What did I do wrong? Did I deserve this?

Confused and broken, I pulled my Bible off the table, and opened it to the psalm that I had studied that morning. I read through it again and just prayed it out loud to the Lord and he answered back in the reading of this Psalm.

Psalm 51

Be merciful to me, O God, be merciful to me, for in you my soul takes refuge; in the shadow of your wings I will take refuge; till the storms of destruction pass by. I cry out to God Most High, to God who fulfills His purpose for me. He will send from heaven and save me; he will put to shame him who tramples on me. Selah God will send out his steadfast love and his faithfulness! My soul is in the midst of lions; I lie down amid fiery beasts - the children of man, whose teeth are spears and arrows, Whose tongues are sharp swords. Be exalted, O God, above the heavens! Let your glory be over all the earth! They set a net for my steps; My soul was bowed down. They dug a pit in my way, But they have fallen into it themselves. Selah My heart is steadfast, O God, My heart is steadfast! I will sing and make melody! Awake, my glory! Awake, O harp and lyre! I will awake the dawn! I will give thanks to you, O Lord, among the peoples; I will sing praises to you among the nations. For your steadfast love is great to the heavens, Your faithfulness to the clouds. Be exalted, O God, above the heavens! Let your glory be over all the earth!"

When I had read this passage earlier in the morning, I had viewed this psalm as a nice reminder of the protection and praise that I should give to the Lord. Lying on the floor in the same spot and reading through this psalm again, I felt the weight of every word as the Lord spoke through this 0salm to me. I could feel every word coming from my heart, but David's words guided me to sharing my emotions and heartbreak. I was seeking a place to hide, and the place I was to hide was under the shadow of His wings. He goes before me, and He would protect me. He had a purpose for me, for my child, for this awful situation. If anyone tried to crush my spirit, He would save me and lift me up.

Even though my soul was being attacked by doubts and pains, this storm was not in my control, and my purpose was to somehow bring glory to the Lord through *every* situation, even painful ones.

My heart is steadfast for the Lord, I will sing because I am grateful for Christ and the eternity he has given me. I will use this situation to bring glory to him. Be exalted, O God, above the heavens! Let your glory be over all the earth!

Reading this psalm took my focus away from the world and put it on my Father above and His purpose. The pain still hurt and nothing would take that away, but my purpose was to use this situation with every tear to glorify the Lord, no matter what the next few days, weeks, months and years held for me.

I ended up going to my doctor that afternoon, where they confirmed that we had lost our child at six weeks and four days, just three days after our first ultrasound. They called it a missed miscarriage. My body had no idea that our child was not alive anymore; it was still expanding, and preparing for the arrival of our sweet baby.

An unexplainable, indescribable numbness came over my body. After a phone call from my doctor on what our next steps were, I decided to wait a few days and see if I could pass our child naturally.

After I took a few long days off work, no baby had made its appearance. The morning sickness continued. I could not grieve because my child was not gone; our child was still there, in my womb. My doctor prescribed a medication to encourage my body to release and deliver our child. The pharmacist warned me that it would feel a lot like labor with hard contractions and stomach aches. I hardly noticed the stomachaches due to the morning sickness that I continued to battle. I took the pills and waited. Minor contractions and bleeding but nothing.

I called my doctor again the next day. She said we could try the medication one more time, so I did. This time contractions were intense and I struggled through the night, eventually passing our child in the morning.

My wonderful doctor asked me to come in about one to two weeks later and check my hormone levels so that she could encourage us in our next steps. So I went and had blood drawn. After blood work and awaiting the results, I went to celebrate Thanksgiving with my family.

While I was on a walk with my mother-in-law, I got an unexpected phone call from my doctor. I had not passed all of the contents in my uterus, and to prevent infection she asked if I would do a D&C.

This was like the nightmare that would not end. Just when I thought it was over, it was not. I could not even grieve my baby because I was still carrying our 11-week-old child, and the process was so heartbreaking.

My husband and I agreed to go ahead with the D&C the next morning. We returned to his parent's home to have our family Thanksgiving, even though my mind was elsewhere. I vividly remember that night. I listened to a distant relative converse about a new baby that was to be born on the other side of my family. I could hear the joy and excitement in each word as they spoke of awaiting this new life. I felt the occasional look from people who knew my situation and glanced over as if to check on me, but I just withdrew inside of myself. I could feel the emotions building.

I excused myself, went outside alone, and lost it. I wanted this whole dream to be over. I wanted to hold my belly and know that one day that baby would kick back but our child never would. Our child was already in Heaven with Jesus, and I was left with an almost empty womb.

I went back inside and had a minimal presence the remainder of the night. We returned home to try to get some sleep before the procedure the next day. The next morning came too soon. We checked in; I got in a gown and waited. More waiting. I have had surgeries before, but something about this one made me feel exposed and broken. I will never forget as they wheeled me into the cold room how I broke down in tears and bawled.

The male nurse said, "I need you to think happy thoughts and count backwards for me." *10 . . . How could I think happy thoughts? 9 . . . Does he know what this procedure is? 8 . . . Good thoughts . . . God somehow has this in his control and someday I will hold my baby. 7 . . .*

Next thing I knew I woke up, and it was over. I immediately started crying again. I remember seeing a nurse switch places with my original nurse, and I thought it was odd, but did not think too much about it. She held my hand and said that she was sorry.

I do not remember much of our conversation but she had mentioned that she had a miscarriage, and this was a very difficult situation. She sat with me until my husband was brought back to be with me. This unnamed nurse was one of the many people that God put in my path to have divine conversations with me in this dark time.

My womb was completely empty, my arms were empty, and my heart was broken. The next few weeks, I did not even bother putting on mascara because it would just irritate my eyes when I would tear up or when my eyes would become swollen from complete meltdowns. God created us with such a specific design so that even our tears have a purpose.

We have two types of tears that are ninety-eight percent water and are used to lubricate the eye or eliminate vapors or toxins from entering the eye, but the third type is different. The third type is comprised of emotional tears that release stress hormones from the body. At the same time, these tears trigger hormones in your body like oxytocin, which allows us to feel connected to others, and endorphins, which are natural pain relievers [5]. After a miscarriage, connection and relief is exactly what I needed. However, this would give me relief for moments, but I was quickly back to feeling this aching hole in my chest.

My doctor reassured me that it was not my fault and that miscarriages happen all the time for unknown reasons. As much as I wanted to just accept the unknown, I *know* who gives life and that same person also has the power to take it away. I know the all-powerful, sovereign, all-knowing God could have saved my child but did not. But why? *Why did he take this life from me? What did I do wrong? What is He trying to teach me? Would I ever have a child? What kind of God hears a woman crying out for a child for years, gives her one, and before she can even hold the child, He takes that sweet precious life away?*

As I battled through this terrible time of grief, I read in the book of Matthew. Matthew was a Jewish man who was an apostle of Jesus Christ. He followed and watched Jesus throughout his life. He was also part of the Jewish community growing up. A portion of scripture that clung to me was through the story of Jesus's early childhood.

Let's go back to the time of King Herod, the wise men, and Jesus. King Herod was a jealous, power-hungry, and selfish king. He wanted to be in power so badly that to prevent his sons from being king, he had them killed. He plotted against anyone who threatened his power. After Jesus's birth in the town of Bethlehem, King Herod came into contact with the wise men who had traveled to visit Jesus because they had heard he was the long-awaited Messiah, the King. Herod asked them to come back by his palace after visiting Jesus to report his location so that he also could go worship the one true king. Of course, this was a trick to find the location for Jesus and to have him killed.

The all-knowing God guided the wise men home through an alternate route so they could avoid running into King Herod. So, what did power-hungry King Herod do? He did not want anyone ruling besides him, so he ordered that all the sons under the age of two should be killed. An angel was sent to Joseph, Mary's husband, to move his family to a safe region, so they left.

However, King Herod followed through with his order to kill all sons under the age of two in Bethlehem.

Then Herod, when he saw that he had been tricked by the wise men, became furious, and he sent and killed all the male children in Bethlehem and in all that region who were two years old or under, according to the time that he had ascertained from the wise men. Then was fulfilled what was spoken by the prophet Jeremiah: A voice was heard in Ramah, weeping and loud lamentation, Rachel weeping for her children; she refused to be comforted, because they are no more. —Matthew 2:16–18

These verses clung to me. Those women, who had done nothing wrong, who were just waiting for their Messiah, lost their sons. How did *all* those women still turn around and worship God? How did they trust in his plan? Verse 18 answers that question. Rachel is the name that refers to all Jewish women. It shows the brutal emotions that these women felt with the loss of their sons. Although this is a brief verse, I felt the weight of each death of a child being outside of their control. The weeping, sorrow, and grief were so loud that I could practically hear the emotions through the words on the page. So many times I refused to be comforted and just wanted to sit in my sorrow. After this verse, the women and the children who were lost were not spoken of again.

Matthew 2:18 is a reference from a passage in the book of Jeremiah. Jeremiah was written to the Jews who were in exile for worshiping other gods than the one true God. They faced many trials, disciplines, and hardships, but God used these circumstances to shape them for His plan and His glory. This specific passage this verse is from is called *"The Lord Will Turn Mourning to Joy."* The passage Matthew is referring to is Jeremiah 31:15–18:

Thus says the Lord: "A voice is heard in Ramah, lamentation and bitter weeping. Rachel is weeping for her children; she refuses to be comforted for her children, because they are no more." Thus says the Lord: "Keep your voice from weeping, and your eyes from tears, for there is a reward for your work," declares the Lord, "and they shall come back from the land of the enemy. There is hope for your future, "declares the Lord, "and your children shall come back to their own country. I have heard Ephraim grieving, 'You have disciplined me, and I was disciplined, like an untrained calf; bring me back that I may be restored, for you are the Lord my God.'"

Verse 16 from the Jeremiah passage is the same as the one from Matthew, but the following two verses continued the story and reminded the Jewish women of three things. One, there is a reward for the work they do on this Earth. He was not referring to salvation since no one can work for their salvation, but he referred to the reward that will be waiting in heaven.

The second thing, He reminded the women of was their hope for the future. At the time, they were waiting for a Messiah, someone to set them free from their bondage of sin and their eternal destiny of Hell. This verse reminded them of the plan that His son would come. It is all part of God's sovereign plan to bring His children home to be with Him eternally. God's plan is greater than humans are! Finally, these verses show that the tribe (Ephraim) was grieving. The verse describes the trial as discipline.

This kind of discipline will mold our spirits into being like Christ and will restore us. This does not happen because it is easy or because the grief goes away, but because we are serving the Lord God. These three thoughts can change our focus from the here and now to the later and forever. They can turn our mind away from the pain to focus on the healer and His plan.

Jewish women of this time had heard that a Messiah would come and would save them. These women were waiting for a savior to relieve them from their sins; they had not known about Jesus's death and resurrection, and that was their hope for the future. We know of Jesus Christ's ultimate sacrifice, but we have a hope for His plans to come again where we will live eternally with him.

And I heard a loud voice from the throne saying, "Look! God's dwelling place is now among the people, and he will dwell with them. They will be his people, and God himself will be with them and be their God. He will wipe every tear from their eyes. There will be no more death or mourning or crying or pain, for the old order of things has passed away. He who was seated on the throne said, "I am making everything new!" Then he said, "Write this down, for these words are trustworthy and true." —Revelation 21:3–5

We know Jesus came, we know he will come again, and we know He will make all things right. There will be no more death, no more pain, and no more tears. God is worth the wait, worth the pain. His plan is worth the suffering that this world offers.

Questions for Reflection:

In what part of your journey have you experienced loss and pain?

____

____

What has happened along your journey that has seemed unfair?

____

____

What is your hope?

____

____

Is there a part of your journey when you wondered if God was there or why this situation was happening?

____

____

What helped you turn your eyes back to Christ and His plan?

____

____

Secret Club Member: Cheri Gilstrap

My Story:

I grew up in a very dysfunctional home. It was filled with violence and alcoholism. In today's terms, it would be called a closed circle. No one came into our home and no information about our home left.

Before Rick and I were married, my childhood doctor told me that I would not be able to have children, to which I made no comment.

During my first pregnancy, Rick had left for the military in California. I was working for a nurse as a nanny. When she came home one afternoon, I told her what had happened. She took me to a doctor who told me I had just experienced an instantaneous abortion.

All I knew was that my baby was gone, just gone. I did not ask any questions; that would not change anything.

My nurse employer took me home and that was that. I told Rick but we did not talk about it much. That is the only person who knew besides the lady I worked for. I thought about it a lot, but I did not speak about it.

My second pregnancy was life threatening to my baby and me. I lost forty-five pounds in three weeks and was admitted to the military hospital where Rick was stationed. It was a cold and sterile environment with military women as nurses. They seemed indifferent and unconcerned about the girls there. We had to make our own beds every morning, go to get our own food, and clean up any mess we made. I was confined to bed with IVs everywhere. I asked for blankets several times in the night, and a nurse finally brought me a folded blanket and tossed it on my bed. I was there four weeks and then went home with no counsel from a doctor on what to do.

When our son was born, he was five pounds. I hemorrhaged and was confined to bed. Since we had to go to the nursery to get our babies at feeding time, that was the only time we had them. And since I was not allowed to get up, I was not allowed to hold my son until I stopped bleeding. The day after his birth they used him to teach the girls how to change and bath their babies. He was so tiny and pitiful, screaming the whole time.

That afternoon I got up without their permission to go get him, but I passed out and was commanded to stay in bed. Not long after, a nurse brought him to me, smiled, and handed him to me, my tiny baby boy, my son. We had both made it through. We were finally "discharged."

Home felt good but this tiny baby, now four pounds, would go back to the hospital many times and would have several serious surgeries. He could not hold food and losing weight fast, he was finally admitted back into the hospital where he caught pneumonia and nearly died. Truly, he is our miracle.

My third pregnancy was also during our military stay. At a normal monthly check-up, the doctor measured me, fifth month, normal so far. He listened for the heartbeat, stood and left the room. When he returned, he said in a flat tone, "There is no heartbeat, the 'fetus' [I hate that word, it was my *baby*] is dead." He told me that a nurse would schedule me for surgery the next day. I said nothing and drove home. After the surgery, the same doctor came into my curtained bedside and said, "Everything is taken care of, you can go home now."

He turned and asked if I wanted to know what "it" was. I was stunned and could not speak; he was obviously annoyed and blurted out, "female" and left. I went home and did not speak of this for many years.

My fourth pregnancy ended at three months. I just did what I was told, no questions, no comments. By my fifth pregnancy we had found a caring doctor who wanted to help us carry this child to full term. All his efforts were in vain, and I found myself on the exam table with him telling me how sorry he was. When they opened the door to my room, I saw a nurse roll a machine out of the room across from me. An abortion . . . across the hall. Another woman not want her baby? How could it be?

I cried all the way home. I cried for days and then had a complete hysterectomy due to massive abdominal scarring.

I knew God had our babies, and we would meet them one day, but I wanted them. I needed them. I love them. To this very day I feel deep pain and sadness because of what I felt was stolen from us. No names, no birth dates, no gravesites, no memorials. They did not do that then. We just went home with unspeakable emptiness and loss.

I could write much more, and I still cry. I do thank God for the hope and healing only He can give us. We will see the babies one day. Little girls? Do they have daddy's curly hairs? Oh, I hope so! Little boys? Wouldn't that be grand!

We do not have names, no songs to sing to them, no nursery rhymes. We just know that God is faithful and only He knows what we never said, our secret thoughts and how it hurt.

My husband Rick carried the weight of the loss I felt with me. I was never alone in this terrible journey. He lost too.

What would you say to a woman who is going through a similar situation?

Today, many, many, many years after . . . I still have moments when tears are the only words. I would tell young women, come talk to me. Tell me what you feel, what you are afraid of, what your dreams were. I would love to listen. I truly understand your broken heart. You do not have to rush to "closure" and you do not have to be silent. I would move close and put my arm around you and let you cry.

Chapter 5 - Beauty in A Thorn

Because of all my adversaries I have become a reproach, especially to my neighbors, and an object of dread to my acquaintances; those who see me in the street flee from me. I have been forgotten like one who is dead; I have become like a broken vessel. For I hear the whispering of many—terror on every side! —as they scheme together against me, as they plot to take my life. —Psalm 31:11–13

I was living every day with puffy eyes and wearing no makeup because what was the point? My emotions and attitude would change on a dime. One minute, I would be making strides at work, and the next, I would be giving myself a pep talk in the mirror to keep myself from crying profusely.

If I was outdoors and I would start to feel a tear, I would try to avoid eye contact with anyone, bat my eyes, and keep moving. If anyone asked or noticed, I would shrug it off as allergies or my contact just dried up. I felt if I drew attention to it, it would make people feel uncomfortable or maybe even irritated that I was once again crying.

Most of the time, the emotions and thoughts came from everyday things, and my thoughts would spider web and connect whatever I was doing to our little one. This child, this desire to be a mother, this loss, felt like a thorn in my body that was always painful, but at times it would get twisted or pushed in deeper. Would I carry this forever?

Thorns are first brought up in the Bible in Genesis, in the Garden of Eden, after the sin of humans.

And to Adam [He] said, "Because you have listened to the voice of your wife and have eaten of the tree of which I commanded you, 'You shall not eat of it,' cursed is the ground because of you; in pain you shall eat of it all the days of your life; thorns and thistles it shall bring forth for you; and you shall eat the plants of the field." —Genesis 3:18

Can you imagine what the Garden of Eden was like? Everything Adam and Eve needed was provided. They had no worries, no concerns, no competition, and no pains. They had an uninterrupted relationship with God.

Of course, we know that this garden was broken due to Satan and a sin that ruined everything. In this conversation with Adam, God was saying the earth would no longer only bring fruit; it would also bring thorns and thistles. God was referring to humans' source of food, but he is also referring to life and struggles on earth. It would no longer be only fruitful; there would be struggles, death, and pain that this earth would hold, burdens because of sin.

We will have cares, concerns, worries, pleasures and desires that belong to this earth that we will carry in and throughout our lives. They will be our "thorns".

Later in the New Testament, Paul talked about the burden that he carried and referred to it as the "thorn in his flesh":

"So to keep me from becoming conceited because of the surpassing greatness of the revelations, ***a thorn was given me in the flesh,*** *a messenger of Satan to harass me, to keep me from becoming conceited. Three times I pleaded with the Lord about this, that it should leave me" (2 Corinthians 12:7–10, emphasis added).*

The Bible does not clearly tell us what Paul's thorn was, but some believe that he had a vision problem or some sort of eye disease that progressed during his ministry. Paul was a messenger of the Lord, and his thorn was something that affected his health, but God did not let it stunt Paul's ministry. Paul talked about his thorn in such a profound way. He knew that God had given him the thorn.

On so many days I have questioned, "Why? Why would God give me not only the thorn of infertility for three years, but then a miscarriage where I felt the weight and loss of a dream that I had for so many years?" It felt so unfair.

A story came to my attention as I struggled through this battle of understanding why God gave me this thorn and how I felt undeserving of it. Job was blameless and upright in the eyes of the Lord. In my standards, he would be good . . . he had a large family, lots of land, and thousands of livestock. He was considered the greatest man in the east.

God allowed a trial to come upon Job, and his wealth, family, and health were taken from him to see if he would still glorify God. Job was sent through an extreme low where all at once, he lost everything and everyone in his life. He was in such grief that he just sat in a pile of ash for days. Job finally cried out to the Lord, asking why he had born, if to experience such darkness. He ended his first plea to the Lord with:

"I am not at ease, nor am I quiet; I have no rest, but trouble comes" (Job 3:26).

Job recognized that although this trial was miserable, he would not let go of his pursuit of God. He was bitter and pronounced that he would stay bitter as long as he was breathing, but he would not disgrace God.

People came with bad advice and questions. Job continued to

ask God why this happened, and God finally responded:

Where were you when I laid the foundation of the earth? Tell me, if you have understanding. Who determined its measurements - surely you know! Or who stretched the line upon it? On what where its bases sunk, Or who laid its cornerstone, When the morning stars sang together And all the sons of God shouted for joy? Or who shut in the sea with doors When it burst out from the womb, When I made clouds its garment And thick darkness its swaddling band, And prescribed limits for it and set bars and doors, And said, Thus far shall you come, and no further, And here shall your proud waves be stayed? (Job 38:4–11)

God ended His questions in chapter 40 of Job stating: *"Shall a faultfinder contend with the Almighty? He who argues with God, let him answer it" (v. 2).*

Many times I questioned God and His plan. I justified to Him that I am *a good person* and did not deserve any of this. At other times I would see a sixteen-year-old who did not even want a child and was blessed with one. I tried to rationalize to God that I was better. I questioned God to gain understanding, but was humbled by the story of Job. God reminded him, and he reminded me, that He is so much bigger than this situation. God knows the measurements of the earth, He has a purpose for the waves and shorelines, and He takes care of the creatures on this earth. If I think for a moment that He needs to explain himself to me, I have forgotten my place and how big and all knowing the God I worship is.

Job concluded his conversation with God:

"Then Job answered the Lord and said: I know that you can do all things, And that no purpose of yours can be thwarted. Who is this that hides counsel without knowledge? Therefore, I have uttered what I did

not understand, Things too wonderful for me, which I did not know. Hear and I will speak; I will question you and you make it known to me. I had heard of you by the hearing of the ear, But now my eyes sees you; Therefore I despise myself, And repent in dust and ashes" (Job 42:1–6).

This does not mean I cannot be sad or grieve; it was a reminder that I do not get to question God as though He needs to justify His actions to me. His plan is greater than I am. He wants to use this trial to draw me closer to Him and to glorify His name.

Back to the story of Paul, Paul perceived that his thorn was given by God but he did not shy away from the statement that Satan tried to use it to get the best of him: *"A messenger of Satan to harass me."*

Satan had reigned over this earth and had a goal to take that thorn and twist it to lead to my destruction. He wanted to see me isolated and trapped and bogged down, because if he could do that, he would have taken my eyes off of the One who is shaping my spirit.

As for you, you meant evil against me, but God meant it for good . . .
— Genesis 50:20

Thorns have two purposes. One is for your destruction. Satan wants to turn your thorn into your downfall. Satan wanted me to be trapped in my emotions and break relationships so I was isolated and vulnerable. He wanted me to have harsh conversations with people. Satan wants us to focus on our thorns and our weaknesses and make life all about us.

Right after we found out that we lost our baby, I went back to work, still carrying with me this lost life in my womb. I did not think staying at home alone would be healthy for me since Kyle was at work. I decided that the Lord had me in this position for a reason, and even if it hurt, I would be honest with others about what I was going through and just see what happened.

I was not sure how the Lord would use it. I told him, "You know my emotional state, you know that talking about this makes me cry and sometimes, I have unstoppable emotions. I give them to you, use me Lord."

As I went on with my mornings, making copies, a number of women came around me not knowing anything about my situation and asked questions like, "Do you have any plans for this weekend? Or how are you doing?"

Remembering my conversation with the Lord I responded with my *real* situation. I would respond honestly, "This weekend I am going to try a few medications to pass my baby since it is not living anymore."

I would tear up, but nothing was uncontrolled. I would not apologize for the tears. I would just let them come.

I was blown away by the responses I received from women. First off, I could not believe the number of women who'd had a miscarriage or struggled with pregnancies or infertility. When I was bold with my story, I could connect on a deeper level. I was able to bring up parts of testimony and freely express my trust in the Lord and the perfection of His timing. Without the boldness of my testimonies, these conversations would have more than likely been something like, "Hi, how are you?" with the response of "Good, have a great day!"

The testimony of God's love and grace would have been lost due to my being scared to share the hard, deep and painful reality.

The thief comes only to steal and kill and destroy; I have come that they may have life, and have it to the full. —John 10:10

Evil still wanted to break me, so he sent people who told me terrible stories about miscarriages and people who made rude and ridiculous comments. Each time I shared my story though, I had two options. I could view it as a chance to share the trial that I was going through and the peace God had given me, or I had the option to shut down the conversation because I did not like how someone worded the never-perfect question or comment about family planning. I was reminded that God uses broken people and broken hearts to show his undoubtable strength and unwavering peace.

Just like my struggle with conceiving a child, I was once again in a situation where people did not know how to talk to me. They did not know what to say, how to comfort me, or what to do. When we were around people who did not know that we had lost a child or had been trying for years to have a family, they would make comments about our family planning or ask when we were going to have children, *as if it were our choice on the timing*.

I was not sure how to respond, so I would just say it was in the Lord's timing and leave it at that. I could feel my thorn getting pushed and twisted deeper.

After my response, I would detour the conversation in a different direction and move on physically, but not mentally. These conversations focused my attention back on my thorn, causing me to feel the pain even more, and what was worse, it felt like I was the only one who felt my pain.

A movement was going around Instagram at the time of my miscarriage and recovery called #DontAsk. It encouraged people to stop asking questions like, "Are you going to have children? How many children do you have? When are you going to get married? or Do you want to have children?"

This movement challenged me. If I was really doing what the Lord wanted me to do, why would I be ashamed to answer that question? Even if it provoked pain or a hard answer, why should I be upset at communicating real heartaches and struggles with another human?

Who knows how they may relate or if they may be in need of encouragement themselves. I felt like this movement was another way to isolate people from communicating about the real hard truths. This movement encouraged isolation and silence.

Isolation is a strategy from the devil. If he can isolate a human and build up walls, he does not need much to take down or completely defeat that person. Satan will seek to break away the community and the people that help build you up and challenge you to be more like Christ.

The last sentence of 2 Corinthians 12:10 states, *"I pleaded with the Lord about this, that it should leave me."* All those days and nights I would pray. I would weep and cry out to the Lord to take this thorn from me. An interesting detail that Paul reveals is that he pleaded three times. Why not four or five? I know I have been on my knees over a hundred times . . . but in the Bible numbers have meaning. The number three means complete, divine wholeness. Paul never lost sight of the God who gave him the thorn. Instead, Paul drew close to the one who could complete him and could turn his weakness of the human body into something that would show the strength of the Lord. Do not be confused! This does not mean the Lord will turn your weakness into *your* strength, but in Him alone you take refuge, and your weakness will show God's strength.

If I asked you to close your eyes and think of a thorn, maybe you would think of a Hawthorn tree with giant spikes or a bush of Barberry spikes that are small and clustered. Maybe you picture a rose. A rose is such a beautiful flower that comes in many colors and sizes. Different roses symbolize different meanings like friendship, romance, and sympathy, but all are so elegant, so beautiful. This stunning, simple flower attracts the eye, but what you do not see until you grab hold of that flower are the spikes that line the stem.

I have spent many days questioning, why is *this* my thorn; why cannot I have a different thorn? When researching roses, I wondered, "Why does such a beautiful flower have thorns?" I learned that thorns have multiple purposes—one is to protect against animals that want to eat the rose, and the other is used for growth. A thorn used for protection discourages herbivores from devouring the plant.

My thorn is the same. As much as I feel the pain, it protects me from falling into the hands of the evil one and draws me to the feet of the Lord for strength. The other reason for a thorn is for growth. Roses grow in bushes and in a community. They have thorns to grab onto each other and facilitate growth. They use their thorns to hook and then grow together. Just like roses, our thorns are meant to be seen and used in our community to allow growth. Others around you have a similar thorn. They need your vulnerability and encouragement for growth. If a rose is not grafted or growing, the rose will not bloom. The flower of the rose is where you see its beauty.

When you focus on the thorns of a rose, you miss the beauty. The same is true for our thorns. When I focus on the thorn of infertility/miscarriage and the sting of those thorns, I miss the beauty of the Lord—The beauty of His grace, His strength, and His plan.

"And we know that for those who love God all things work together for good, for those who are called according to ***his*** *purpose" (Romans 8:28, emphasis added).*

In Luke, Jesus tells a parable about seeds, and He talks about a seed/person who knows Christ and starts to grow but gets choked up by the thorns. Such a person focuses on the pains, pleasures, and desires of this world instead of seeing the beauty of Christ. At times, I felt like if I were not careful, I would start to doubt God, turning my focus on those prickly thorns and the pain that I was going through. God will help you see past your thorns if you just ask.

Sometimes I would miss pausing and seeking God. I would go through my day and start to struggle with doubt or be let down by others, and I would forget that I have an entire Bible filled with God's words and stories to help me through any time and any season.

Some days I felt overdone with the weight of our waiting, and losing a child would be too much for me. I would pray, "Take this thorn from me Lord." As much as I wanted the weight of this thorn gone, is that what I should have been asking the Lord?

Paul didn't end his plea to the Lord with "take this thorn" instead he continued,

"But he said to me, 'My grace is sufficient for you, for my power is made perfect in weakness.' Therefore, I will boast all the more gladly of my weaknesses, so that the power of Christ may rest upon me. For the sake of Christ, then, I am content with weaknesses, insults, hardships, persecutions and calamities. For when I am weak, then I am strong" (2 Corinthians 12:9–10).

He continued to say, "I know that this thorn is a weakness, I know Satan is trying to turn it into my destruction, *but* this weakness draws me to You and for that I will boast. I am content that when I am weak the Lord will show His strength."

Questions for Reflection:

Do you feel overwhelmed by your weakness?

____

____

Have you recognized what your thorn may be?

____

____

How can you change your focus from the thorn to the beautiful flower that the Lord is creating?

____

____

How can you take advantage of the doors he opens for you to share your story and relate to others?

____

____

Secret Club Member: Lois Magnuson

My Story:

In September 1989, Bryan and I were so excited to tell my parents that they were going to be grandparents! We had already planned a trip to Santa Cruz to spend the weekend with them and were thrilled that we would give them the news. After arriving back home, I noticed that something was not right. I called the doctor, and he explained that I was probably having a miscarriage and explained what would happen soon.

How could something that seemed so natural for other women seem to be so difficult for me? I had seen the heartbeat. I saw the tiny body. It was alive inside me. Now what would I say to everyone that we had shared our exciting news with? Would I ever have the joy of pregnancy and birth?

I was adopted. I loved the fact that my parents told me that I was chosen, a gift especially given to them. I loved that I had red hair and no one else in my family did. I loved that I was left-handed and no one else in the family was. I loved that when I became a child of God I was adopted twice. I loved everything about adoption, but I wanted to have the experience of having my own child.

After the miscarriage, the doctor said that miscarriages are very common and a high percentage of first pregnancies end in a miscarriage. So we tried again and not too long after this, we discovered we were pregnant again. Could I have just been in that secret club for a short time? Since we had told so many people early in the first pregnancy, we decided that we would not tell family or friends about this pregnancy until much later.

Eight weeks later, I started to miscarry again. Those feelings and pain came rushing back. The second miscarriage made me feel more alone. Since we didn't tell anyone, we were pregnant, we didn't tell anyone we were losing the baby. Bryan and I cried alone.

When I went back to the doctor I requested to be sent to a specialist. He said specialists were brought in after three miscarriages. I could not imagine having to go through this again, so after discussion, we found a specialist, and he confidently said he would find the trouble and try to resolve it. I felt that God had given me a doctor who knew my struggle and wanted to help me. Looking back, I thank the Lord for directing me to this doctor. The issue was low progesterone, which we were able to manage and then were blessed with three healthy, full-term children.

Is there something that triggers your memory for your lost babies?

After having all three children, I didn't often think about the two I lost except when completing medical forms to list the number of pregnancies. When Skillet came out with their song *Lucy*, it made me think about my two children and them walking hand-in-hand with Jesus. Someday I will see them, and they will know that I was their mommy.

What would you say to someone who is walking journey that is similar to yours?

What do I say to young women who desperately want a child and have struggled with miscarriages and infertility? How do I stand alongside my beautiful daughter and her husband, who would give anything to hold their own precious baby? The answer is, I don't know what to say. I do know it is a walk of faith. It is daily putting our dreams and desires in God's hand. He knows the brokenness. He knows the emptiness. He knows the longing.

Was there a Bible story, song or scripture that encouraged you throughout your journey?

One of my favorite stories in the Bible is the story of Hannah in 1 Samuel 1. After planning all the showers and watching all her friends and family have babies so naturally (my modern translation) and being provoked and irritated by them all, she still understood that God had closed her womb for some purpose. Even her husband, Elkanah, tried to console her by comparing himself to ten sons. She was so distressed that she wept bitterly to the Lord and made a vow to Him if only He would give her a child, "And the Lord remembered her. And in due time Hannah conceived and bore a son, and she called his name Samuel, for she said, 'I have asked for him from the Lord.'"

Hannah followed through with her vow and dedicated Samuel to the Lord. In response, Samuel did mighty things for God. Her heart was exulted in the Lord, and she praised Him for answering her prayer.

God has a plan for us. We do not know what it is, but I am confident He is faithful. It is not always the plan we want but it is the plan He has designed for us to give Him the glory.

Keep trusting. Keep seeking. Keep asking. Weep. Wait. Expect God will act. Celebrate Him when He does!

Chapter 6 - Happiness...? Yeah Right!

But I trust in you, O Lord; I say, "You are my God." My times are in your hand; rescue me from the hand of my enemies and from my persecutors! Make your face shine on your servant; save me in your steadfast love! O Lord, let me not be put to shame, for I call upon you; let the wicked be put to shame; let them go silently to Sheol. Let the lying lips be mute, which speak insolently against the righteous in pride and contempt. — Psalm 31:14–18

"Sensitive," "cry-baby," and "dramatic" are all words that people would pin to me. Ever since I was young, I would easily be overwhelmed with emotions. I could be smiling and laughing one minute, then in tears the next. I would make choices based on how I felt or what would bring me happiness.

As I got older, situations that were happy, sad, or even frustrating would end with one to hundreds of tears streaming down my face. I could guarantee tears shed if I watched a video of soldiers returning to their families, a puppy getting saved, or some random act of kindness. These emotions would just tug on my heartstrings. The music I would listen to could change my emotions in an instant. I would listen to rock and harder beats, and my body would be on edge. I would be more prone to anger and frustration. Once I figured this out about myself, I switched to only listening to worship or encouraging music that would lift my spirits. Worship music allowed me to focus my heart on whom I needed to seek and what my emotion should be. Of course, I listened to the occasional Disney song or soundtrack, but as a whole I wanted my emotions to be controlled and focused on the real things that matter.

After our miscarriage, the music I would listen to opened up my heart every time I was in the car. I could not go through one car ride without being in tears. I would just sing my heart out and cry out to the Lord the lyrics of the songs. I believe that God allowed specific songs to play that allowed me to voice and express the emotions that I was feeling. Sometimes I would even listen to the same songs on repeat because crying felt good. In those moments, I felt like I could be honest with my emotions and the pain that I was experiencing. I even kept an extra container of mascara in the car so that I could put myself back together, and get out of the car ready to move on with my day.

Emotions are not bad. They are the way the body releases stress and feelings. Some emotions are soothing to the body, while others cause harm. Emotions are guided by the rhythm of the heart. When your body starts to experience a situation, your heart adjusts its rhythm. This rhythm signals to the brain how to respond. If you are feeling anger, frustration, irritation, or anxiety, your heart releases an erratic pattern that clouds your brain's ability to work properly and this creates stress on the body. When your body is experiencing stress, your body will make decisions based solely on the heart, which will not allow your brain to process through the actions or make wise decisions. If you are feeling sadness, love, etcetera, your body receives the slow pattern of the heart and blood is pumped to specific parts of the body associated with those feelings.[6] Many times you feel a warm, soft heart during these emotions.

Living and acting only based on emotions can be very dangerous. Trying to find the balance of emotions after a miscarriage is extremely challenging and can end in actions that damage relationships with people and your relationship with

God.

And a great windstorm arose, and the waves were breaking into the boat, so that the boat was already filling. But he was in the stern, asleep on the cushion. And they woke him and said to him, "Teacher, do you not care that we are perishing?" And he awoke and rebuked the wind and said to the sea, "Peace! Be still!" And the wind ceased, and there was a great calm. 40 He said to them, "Why are you so afraid? Have you still no faith?" 41 And they were filled with great fear and said to one another, "Who then is this, that even the wind and the sea obey him? — Mark 4:35–41

I would get so wrapped up in my emotions at times, that I would lose sight of the God I served. Mark 4 shows us valuable lessons that the disciples learned on a boat. The first one was a situation where Jesus was on the boat with the disciples and a storm came. The disciples start to panic, but they noticed that Christ was sleeping during this storm. They got irritated and woke him. Jesus then asked them, *"Why are you afraid, O you of little faith."*

When he mentioned faith, he was not talking about salvation, but the faith of the disciples to depend on Jesus. They accused him of not caring, and Jesus wanted them to recognize that He was not scared or frightened, therefore, they should not feel that way either if they truly knew and understood the man they were sharing the boat with.

During my storm of losing a child, it was easy for me to get irritated with my circumstances and cry out to God, questioning his concern for me. *Do you even hear me? Is this what my life has turned out to be?* I tended to go down a roller coaster of doubt, which would always lead to the thoughts that I was not the woman God created me to be or that I was somehow a mistake. God created us to populate and reproduce. He gave me these instincts to long for and take care of a family, but the dream was stripped from me.

I was sad, grieving, and even jealous. I would make rash decisions that would pull me away from people in my life who were there to help and encourage. I was missing the fact that God was right next to me, in the boat, riding through this storm with me. This miscarriage did not take him by surprise. This storm was not too large for him. He was willing to guide me through it, but he would not take it away. I had to choose whether I wanted to go through the storm by my own efforts of panic, frustration, anger, and anxiety, or if I wanted to seek the peace that the Lord offered.

The option of the Lord's peace would require that I ride out the storm in this boat wherever it was going to take me. When I decided to search for peace and follow Christ's lead, even through this hard storm, it got even more challenging before it got better.

I spent a summer nannying for a family of three. Many of our days in the summer were spent outside playing and running around to enjoy the Midwest weather. One of the popular activities was playing on a yellow and blue seesaw in their backyard. Even though I outweighed all the kids, they still would get on and wait for me to hop on the other side. I would get on the side of the seesaw and my weight would send them into the air. They would smile and laugh, but since I carried more weight than them, unless I made a move, they would stay in the air. I would slowly stand up, allowing the weight to shift so they could sink to the bottom. Then I would sit back down and the cycle would continue until the burn of the workout in my thighs would sting so badly that I had to take a break.

This is what most relationships felt like during grief. I felt as though I had to fake emotions of happiness and the feeling of being okay so that my friends would enjoy their time, but on the inside, I was covering up the weight that was there. This was exhausting and since I did not want to make an uncomfortable situation for my friend, I would not be honest with them or myself. I could feel the weight of my burden, like I would in my thighs after lifting up my own weight over and over again. I would carry the burden until I would shut down and disengage.

Shortly after Kyle and I had our miscarriage, our closest relatives, Kyle's brother, Chris, and his wife, Kara, found out they were pregnant. They wanted to be cautious of our reactions and emotions, so they told us in private. Of course, we showed nothing but happiness for them that evening, but after they left, I remember looking at Kyle on the couch, and him just coming over to hold me. No words could be said.

We were genuinely excited about our new family member and for Chris and Kara. The pain in our flesh from the new thorn that we were carrying dug a little deeper, so in that moment all we could do was cry and pray. We committed to praying for our new niece or nephew every night, for the baby's development, labor, and most of all, that the child would come to know Jesus one day.

As time went on, we watched and celebrated this new life through a gender reveal, many dinners, and family time. Kara and I decided early on to have "elephant in the room" conversations, and she was not afraid to ask me questions about my journey and what I was walking through. She was beyond understanding when I would shed a tear or two, not in harsh emotions but in grief. As time passed, my sorrow for our lost child would still surface, but at other times a sense of frustration and anger also arose.

At Kara's baby shower, I remember watching her open gifts and a feeling of sadness came over me. *I wanted a child, I wanted this. I wanted to have those conversations with other moms about what was about to come; the pain and memory of labor, the joy of holding your child for the first time, the breastfeeding advice, and even the postpartum conversations. I wanted that and I wanted it now.*

I started to shed a tear but quickly wiped my eyes and continued with a smile. But God used this moment to take a hold of me and put the questions in my mind: *What are you sad about? Are you sad about your lost child?*

Yes, of course! Yet, as I thought about it, I changed my mind. Being honest, I had to answer "no." What I felt at that moment was different than grief. I felt more than sadness. I felt underlying anger, frustration, and jealousy. Grief was not why I had shed that tear. Another question came to my mind. *Are you mad that you are not getting your way?*

Bingo! That was it. I was mad and frustrated at God. At His plan. I was watching a baby shower that I wanted from God, and *He* was not giving it to me. I was being provoked by jealousy and my desire for a baby. That's why I had shed that tear. I immediately felt guilt fall over my body, and I realized that this emotion of jealousy and anger at God was sinful. It was hard to admit that to myself and to come to grips that I was a disciple in the boat during a storm. I was panicking and mad at God for putting this storm in my way. All the while, He was there, peacefully sleeping and waiting for me to recognize what He, alone, offers. If I truly knew who God was and His purpose for me, then I would not be riding this emotional roller coaster, sinning against the all-powerful, all-knowing, and perfect God.

That challenging question of, *what are you sad about right now?* changed my life. It helped me to get off the roller coaster of emotions and question my true feelings and planted my feet firmly on the boat. If my answer to the question was sadness due to grief and missing my child, I would let myself cry, and feel the pain. On the other hand, if I was sad because I was not getting my way, I would apologize to God and then seek His peace through the Bible on how to battle this emotion.

Envy could have ruined my relationship with Kara even though the battle I faced was actually with God. Satan wants to isolate us from people and our communities that would point us to Christ. The question became, "How can I go out of my way to show Kara and to show others how God can use broken people to build relationships and share his glory?"

On September 27th, 2019, my sweet nephew, Paxton Sawyer, was born. As we prepared to see our new nephew, I spent time begging the Lord to take away any emotion that would come as a result of jealousy, anger or frustration. I did not want my emotions to take the focus off Paxton, Kara, and Chris. I knew that throughout the whole day I would battle thoughts and emotions, but with the Lord next to me, I was ready. As I walked into that hospital room, I was completely overwhelmed by joy when I saw this new little family of three.

Wasn't I happy? Sure, I was happy, but what I prayed for was to not have a selfish heart. Our culture tends to confuse the two. According to the dictionary and common English, happiness and joy are synonyms. According to the Bible, though, they are very different. Happiness is a feeling that comes over you when you know life is good and you cannot help but smile. The Bible describes joy as given by God. Kay Warren writes, "Joy is the settled assurance that God is in control of all the details of my life, the quiet confidence that everything is going to be alright and a determined choice to praise God in every situation."[7]

One of the magnificent rewards of studying the Bible is seeing people like you and me who may go through hard, strenuous, life-threatening situations, but in the end, they are filled with joy. Paul, an ambassador of Christ, was thrown in prison for his beliefs. Yet, Paul continued to work for the Lord's glory in a prison and brought many people to Christ. David was the rightful king of Israel and was pursued by Saul, the current ruler of Israel. David knew God had chosen him, but he did not know God's day-by-day plan, so despite the circumstances, David knew God would not abandon him. In Psalm 16, verse 11 David said, *"You make known to me the path of life; in your presence there is fullness of joy; at your right hand are pleasures forevermore."*

Despite what I think would make me happy—the American dream, the family of five, the

feelings of pregnancy or being a mother—I know that God has not forgotten about me and has a plan for my life. I need to stop fighting Him for control. He knows my path; He is there to give me joy even in tough situations, and following Him will result in pleasures beyond what I can imagine. Even though my heart hurt several times while serving my sister- and brother-in-law, I knew that God would continue to give me joy. God would keep my emotions under control, as long as I endured this storm and sought His peace.

Therefore, since we are surrounded by so great a cloud of witnesses, let us also lay aside every weight, and sin which clings so closely, and let us run with endurance the race that is set before us, looking to Jesus, the founder and perfecter of our faith, who for the joy that was set before him endured the cross, despising the shame, and is seated at the right hand of the throne of God. —Hebrews 12:1–2

After the disciples woke Jesus in the boat due to panic, He questioned them about their understanding of who *He* truly was. Jesus then immediately calmed the storm. It was obvious by the disciples' response that they still, after all this time, did not understand who Jesus was.

When my emotions get out of control and I get angry or jealous that God is not giving me what I want, I am forgetting whom He is. At times he may calm the storm, even after emotions that do not deserve to be coddled, but that rarely means that is the end of the trial or the end of that storm. The Lord wants all of His followers to go through trials to learn, grow and take steps of faith, to ultimately bring glory to God's name.

Questions for Reflection:

What is something you do to release the pain of loss or grief?

____

____

List any relationship that has been broken or altered since you started going through this trial?

____

____

What steps can you take to mend those relationships?

____

____

Are there times that you disguise anger and frustration with God as grief?

____

____

Secret Club Member: Emily W.

My Story:

My husband, Geoff, and I had two children, four and two years old. We found out on July 21 that we were pregnant with baby number three. The pregnancy never really felt normal for me, after having two other healthy pregnancies. I was very sick from the beginning—lots of insomnia, nausea, and anxiety. We had normal ultrasounds through the beginning, but at fourteen weeks, I went to the ER for high blood pressure and a rapid heart rate. They ran a lot of tests but could not pinpoint the problem. I went to my primary care doctor and she ran labs and discovered something was wrong with my thyroid.

I was diagnosed with hyperthyroidism but no one could tell me why. As the pregnancy went on, I continued to feel worse. I was tired all the time, even with naps. I would go to bed early and would be exhausted. My breathing was always fast, and I felt out of breath and winded all the time.

Around seventeen weeks, we had the quad-screen, which tests for Down Syndrome, trisomy, neural tube defects, and abdominal wall defects. I got a call that they could not run the test because the values were too high, so I had a redraw, which resulted in a similar error. I was sent to a high-risk OB.

On Nov. 7, 2019, we went to a high-risk OB doctor, who did an ultrasound. The tech was very friendly and talkative at first, but as time passed, she became very reserved and stopped talking. I knew this was not a good sign, from being in and familiar with the medical field. After she left the room, I looked at my husband and told him that I thought something was very wrong based on the technician's behavior.

We were taken into the next room and were told that our

baby probably had triploidy. In a healthy human there are typically two of each chromosome (one from dad and one from mom). In our baby, there were three copies of every chromosome. This condition has too much genetic information and cannot sustain life. Our doctor told us that we had a partial molar pregnancy where there was too much genetic material with the baby, and it was causing problems with me, as well. It explained all my symptoms, and it is very high risk for the mother.

I was referred to a medical center and within one week, I saw five different maternal fetal medicine doctors, and I was hospitalized for three days because of concerning symptoms. We were told that this was very high risk for me, that there was no chance of our baby surviving this, and that legally they could not help us. We went into our appointment on November 14, 2019, and I had more labs done, which showed that my kidneys were failing, my blood pressure was too high, and I was at high risk for stroke, heart attack, or seizure. My doctors were at the point where they had to get approval from the risk management team, ethics team, and medical ICU team for an emergency induction to save maternal life.

We were admitted to the hospital that night, but we needed time to process, so we waited until the next morning to start the induction period. Our baby girl, Katherine MaryAnne, was born at 1:33 p.m. on November 15, 2019. She was born alive at twenty weeks and four days. Within fifteen to twenty minutes, I was rushed to emergency surgery for bleeding. My husband and parents held her until I returned. Once I was out of surgery, she laid on my husband's chest and my chest until she passed away just after 4:00 p.m.

I became compelled to share my story because of how traumatic this part of our journey was. Losing a baby after having two healthy pregnancies was unexpected, and I know too many other women who suffer in silence. I was grateful I had people to reach out to for advice and help with navigating this event with two children. You do not understand what it is like to be in "the loss" club until you are forced to be part of it. It is incredibly lonely.

Is there a scripture that stuck out to you during your journey?

People would say, "You are so brave" or "I don't think I could have made it through what you did." Coming up with a response to those statements was hard because this part of my journey was not a choice. It was the hand I was dealt. I put one foot in front of the other because I had to. At times I found myself asking, *why me? Why do I have to go through this?* In the book of Esther, after she became queen, she had the opportunity to step out and stand firm for her people, but she also risked being killed for taking her concerns to the king. Her cousin Mordecai told her, "For if you remain silent at this time, relief and deliverance for the Jews will arise from another place, but you and your father's family will perish. And who knows but that you have come to a royal position **for such a time as this?" (**Esther 4:1)

Those words struck me: *for such a time as this.* I had been placed in this moment at this time in my life, and it was not a mistake or accident. Over time, I felt the question turn from *why me* to *why not me?* I realized that I had the right care and support team to guide and carry me through this hard and traumatic time. I felt as though everything in my life had prepared me for this very part of my journey. I have felt compelled to share my story so that one day, if needed, I can help walk someone else through their own journey.

What does your family do to celebrate Katherine's life?

On her birthday, we hope to do a service project as a family to serve others. This past year, with COVID-19, we did a cookie drop. We baked cookies and dropped them off at family member's homes. In the future, I hope it looks like us serving at the Ronald McDonald homes, serving others who have loved ones in the hospital. Each year our celebration of Katherine's life may look different, and that is ok. Changes do not mean that her life means any less.

Katherine's name is known and talked about regularly in our home. Our now-five-year-old daughter remembers vividly holding her sister and brings up the memory sporadically. We keep her ashes on our mantle and have pictures in our home.

What would you say to someone who was walking a similar journey to you?

Neither my husband nor I had ever lost an immediate family or had dealt with real, deep grief. A couple came by our home the night after Katherine passed away. We were reluctant to have them visit at first because we did not know if we were up for visitors, but the words they spoke to us were a blessing and exactly what we needed to hear. They told us that grief does not follow seven steps like people think it should. It is more like waves. Some of the large waves you are prepared for and they do not knock you over, but the undertow can sweep you off your feet.

On Katherine's due date, I was prepared for a rough day. When the day came I was, of course, sad, but I was okay. I stood firm as that day came and went. However, when Mother's Day arrived, I was not prepared and did not expect it to hit me so hard on a day that I had celebrated before. My whole identity as a mother was changed, and it swept me off my feet. Being told by a couple who knew and could relate with the grief that we were experiences. They told us that, "Feelings were just going to come and to take them as so instead of expecting a perfect pattern or certain steps." This was exactly what we needed to hear.

Chapter 7 - What Do I Do Now?

Oh, how abundant is your goodness, which you have stored up for those who fear you and worked for those who take refuge in you, in the sight of the children of mankind! In the cover of your presence you hide them from the plots of men; you store them in your shelter from the strife of tongues. Blessed be the Lord, for he has wondrously shown his steadfast love to me when I was in a besieged city. I had said in my alarm, "I am cut off from your sight." But you heard the voice of my pleas for mercy when I cried to you for help. — Psalm 31:19–22

Here I am, four-and-a-half years after we started trying for a child. It has been two-and-a- half years since my miscarriage and we are still waiting. After our miscarriage, I would pray to the Lord for understanding, for Him to open my eyes because I did not understand. Over time, He did just that. My pregnancy two-and-a-half years ago was in fact an answer to prayer, just not the answer my eyes were looking for. Before our pregnancy, we were unsure if we were able to get pregnant due to the time it was taking, the blood tests and panels showed nothing wrong with our systems. After the intense stage of grieving our child, we both found peace to our worries of being able to conceive. Yes, we could get pregnant. After our miscarriage people told us there would be a high chance of getting pregnant again. We prayed that this would be true, but we once again felt that God was telling us to wait. I trusted Him; God had given us a new life without any medical intervention and we would wait on Him again.

God opened my eyes to the women all around me who were suffering from isolation and heartbreak. They were lost in the exact secret, confusing battle of infertility and miscarriages. So many women pushed this battle to the back of their lives and held it inside where it would eat away at them. While they looked normal on the outside, this secret was consumed so much of them, but is hidden due to fears of vulnerability until a woman is bold enough to share a glimpse of it. This creates an opportunity for women to open up, share, and connect on a truly special level.

God put women in my own life to encourage me during these hard, secret times where only God knew what I needed, women like Melanie Erks, Katelyn Skillman, my mom, and family. Some of these women did not even know they were helping but their transparency of their own struggles and lives encouraged, guided and helped me share my thorn and continue to grow. It encouraged me to be as transparent with other women who asked a normal question that had an abnormal answer instead of just moving on with my day. One in four women have had a miscarriage, and one in eight women have struggled with getting pregnant. That is so many women who belong to this secret club. All these women carry the same thorn, and instead of sharing, their own story stays hidden and they cover the pain. My heart ached for these women.

While I was in this period of waiting, I would question, "Lord, what is my step that I should take?"

I felt instruction from God through my quiet study time that I should write a book about my journey. I almost laughed about it when I first thought about it. I am a person who can count on one hand how many complete books I have read cover to cover. I was the kid who slept through English class because reading made me tired. I was completely unqualified and uncomfortable with the idea.

Everything, and I mean everything, kept pointing to this step of writing a book. Every sermon, every song, all my quiet study times—it kept coming to mind. God once again, used His Word to encourage my step.

Steps are scary. They are hard to understand, but the best feeling is knowing and following the Lord. It gives you the ability to use your situation to glorify the Lord instead of yourself.

A common story of the Bible was an encouragement to me as I went through this time of questioning whether or not this was the step for me.

Immediately He [Jesus] made the disciples get into the boat and go before him to the other side, while he dismissed the crowds. And after he had dismissed the crowds, he went up on the mountain by himself to pray. When evening came, he was there alone, but the boat by this time was a long way from the land, beaten by the waves, for the wind was against them. And in the fourth watch of the night[c] he came to them, walking on the sea. But when the disciples saw him walking on the sea, they were terrified, and said, "It is a ghost!" and they cried out in fear. But immediately Jesus spoke to them, saying, "Take heart; it is I. Do not be afraid." And Peter answered him, "Lord, if it is you, command me to come to you on the water." He said, "Come." So Peter got out of the boat and walked on the water and came to Jesus. But when he saw the wind, he was afraid, and beginning to sink he cried out, "Lord, save me." Jesus immediately reached out his hand and took hold of him, saying to him, "O you of little faith, why did you doubt?" And when they got into the boat, the wind ceased. And those in the boat worshiped him, saying, "Truly you are the Son of God."— Matthew 14:22–33

The disciples were *back in the boat*! They were going through yet another storm (the first storm was discussed in the last chapter). I could relate to this on every level. I had waited for years to get pregnant and then after my miscarriage, my instruction was to once again wait. My storm was the same battle as before. I was worn out and tired of waiting, but this time, like the disciples, things were different.

This time on the boat, instead of Jesus being there sleeping, He was back on the shore and did not go to sea with them. They were alone and with only each other. In the first storm, Jesus just wanted them to stay focused on him, not the storm, and to have peace that his plan was greater.

This time, though, was different because Peter was not asked to just have peace, but to actually get out of the boat and walk on the rough waves with steps of faith towards Jesus.

The mission changed from the internal struggle of being controlled by emotions to actually showing and demonstrating the faith that he believed in.

When I said OK to the Lord about writing this book, I expected Him to calm the storm, but just like when Peter stepped out of the boat, He did not stop the waves. When Peter first stepped out of the boat, his eyes were locked on Jesus. I am still waiting for a child while I am being asked to take this step of writing a book. The emotional struggles are still there—the grief, the battles are still present—but they are not my focus, Jesus is. I decided to take a step, *OK Lord, I am going to do this but I need you. I need you to guide my pen and my thoughts and lead me through these next steps.*

There is a point when Peter takes a step or two, and he looks down at his feet then starts to sink. There were moments of my doubting the instruction and guidance of the Lord. I was focusing on my feet and where I thought I should go in reference to this storm. Instead, Jesus wanted me to look to him and know that He will place my feet on a safe path that glorifies Him. The Lord uses people to encourage, but Satan also uses the flesh of people to discourage. Random people, as I started drafting my book, said some discouraging things that put my writing on hold. I felt unqualified, and it made me doubt my ability and God's step for me.

The Lord kindly reminded me that he uses people who are unqualified so that the outcome glorifies Him. He uses people who are nobody and looked down upon so they can testify that they could not have done it without Christ. I battled those comments and thoughts through this entire journey. I was reminded that God will not ask me to do something to then have me fail.

My other biggest barrier that the evil one tried to use was time and distractions. I love to nap, sleep, and spend time with people. Therefore, I had all the distractions in the world to overcome. It would challenge my self-discipline and my time management. Then, when I would sit down and write, I would just feel at ease and like I was exactly where I was supposed to be.

When I did not know how to do something or write something, I would pray and study His word. I would then see or feel in the strangest way through the Holy Spirit, God continuing to guide me even through little details of this book.

All people who are Christ followers have a time or several times in their lives when their faith in Christ is tested and they are asked to show obedience by doing things that seem crazy to the outside world. Christ followers, though, are living for an eternal world and not this one. Their reward is in heaven, and their love for God is worth any sort of sacrifice requested of them in this world.

Hebrews 13, the hall of faith chapter, walks through so many examples of ordinary people who took some small and giant steps of faith in God, steps that showed the work of God.

By faith Noah, when warned about things not yet seen, in holy fear built an ark to save his family. By his faith he condemned the world and became heir of the righteousness that is in keeping with faith. By faith Abraham, when called to go to a place he would later receive as his inheritance, obeyed and went, even though he did not know where he was going. By faith he made his home in the promised land like a stranger in a foreign country; he lived in tents, as did Isaac and Jacob, who were heirs with him of the same promise . . . And by faith even Sarah, who was past childbearing age, was enabled to bear children because she considered him faithful who had made the promise.

By faith Abraham, when God tested him, offered Isaac as a sacrifice. He who had embraced the promises was about to sacrifice his one and only son, even though God had said to him, "It is through Isaac that your offspring will be reckoned." Abraham reasoned that God could even raise the dead, and so in a manner of speaking he did receive Isaac back from death.

By faith Isaac blessed Jacob and Esau in regard to their future. By faith Jacob, when he was dying, blessed each of Joseph's sons, and worshiped as he leaned on the top of his staff. By faith Joseph, when his end was near, spoke about the exodus of the Israelites from Egypt and gave instructions concerning the burial of his bones. By faith Moses' parents hid him for three months after he was born, because they saw he was no ordinary child, and they were not afraid of the king's edict. By faith Moses, when he had grown up, refused to be known as the son of Pharaoh's daughter. He chose to be mistreated along with the people of God rather than to enjoy the fleeting pleasures of sin. He regarded disgrace for the sake of Christ as of greater value than the treasures of Egypt, because he was looking ahead to his reward. By faith he left Egypt, not fearing the king's anger; he persevered because he saw him who is invisible. By faith he kept the Passover and the application of blood, so that the destroyer of the firstborn would not touch the firstborn of Israel.

By faith the people passed through the Red Sea as on dry land; but when the Egyptians tried to do so, they were drowned. By faith the walls of Jericho fell, after the army had marched around them for seven days. By faith the prostitute Rahab, because she welcomed the spies, was not killed with those who were disobedient. — Hebrews 13:7–11, 17–31

All of these statements are common Bible stories that we are familiar with, but together they show a larger picture of how our faith in God for the little and big things are all part of God's plan. Many of these people of faith did not live extraordinary lives filled with all their wants and desires because of following God. Many of them lived the opposite—died hard deaths, lived as nomads, made hard decisions—but all of them continued striving to please and be obedient in each step they took. Why? They took each step because of the promise of eternity with Christ.

These were all commended for their faith, yet none of them received what had been promised, since God had planned something better for us so that only together with us would they be made perfect. — Hebrews 11:39–40

Any step is a step as long as it is focused on Christ. If you take a step that is not focused on Christ, you will sink into the storm.

What is your step that you are being asked to take? Maybe it is something big like Noah building an ark in a land-locked location that had never seen rain. Maybe it is something foreign to you that you are not sure how or why that would work, like embryo adoption, surrogacy, or fostering. Maybe it is an act as small and a simple as Rahab did by hiding spies, which resulted in her family being saved from death. Maybe it is a simple conversation with someone who is hurting or bringing a meal to a family in need. Do not let your lack of obedience result in missed opportunities of revealing and sharing the testimony of God.

As I finish up this step that the Lord has asked from me, there is nothing I would love more than seeing those two pink lines but until then or until my next step, I will wait—not on the hope of humans but on the all-knowing, all-powerful, perfect God.

Love the Lord, all you his saints! The Lord preserves the faithful but abundantly repays the one who acts in pride. Be strong, and let your heart take courage, all you who wait for the Lord! — Psalm 31:24-25

This scripture was dedicated to the child that we lost. He is forever in our hearts! God used such an ugly thorn to make something beautiful that only He could do.

Questions for Reflection

Where have you seen moments of faith in your journey?

Where have you seen long periods that required steadfast faith?

What is your next step?

What is God calling you to do with where you are?

Your Turn

Every person has a story, and now it is your turn to write down yours! Write down in as much detail as you would like, your journey! There is a beauty in writing and reflecting on your story!

What scriptures or songs have encouraged you throughout your journey?

What would you say to a woman who was going through a similar journey as you are going through?

I want you to know that I have prayed for all people who have opened this book. I would love to hear your story and about the step of faith that God has asked and designed specifically for you! Feel free to email me at brianna.lindenmeyer@gmail.com

My Husband

On June 14, 2014, I walked down the aisle to a man who loved God and loved me despite my brokenness and past mistakes. Kyle and I said, "I do" on a windy day in Lawson Missouri. Our wedding was not overly glamorous or focused on details; it was simple and the number one important thing was to marry this man I loved.

Through this journey, there was one person who was always there. He picked me up off the floor, laid with me, took care of me and encouraged me through it all. Kyle never saw our journey of waiting as my problem or his but it was our burden that we would carry and navigate through together.

After we lost our child, it became crystal clear to me just how differently we processed grief. Kyle was strong for me, but I remember times when I would be frustrated because it was not affecting him the same way as me, and it almost seemed as though he did not care but I knew he did. I asked him several questions about our journey of waiting and loss:

What was most difficult for you when we lost our child?

The day that we lost our child was the worst day of my life. I was filled with sadness, and I felt broken for you. I was frustrated because I felt as though it was something we waited a long time for and then God shut the door at the last minute. After the door was shut, it was a challenge to continue to follow God's direction. I also struggled to have the patience for Him to allow us to get pregnant again.

Do you ever think about our lost child?

I do not think about our child regularly, but I am more sympathetic when other people go through a miscarriage because I know how hard it is. Losing a child completely changed my outlook on the common occurrence of a miscarriage. I have always supported pro-life but the weight of this miscarriage helped me to understand, at a deeper level, the value of life. It angers me more when people go the other way. I am definitely more passionate and outspoken about the loss of a baby before birth.

What did you find encouraging?

People came over and prayed for us and continued to pray through our journey.

As we continue to wait for God to guide our steps, I know that I would not be in the place I am without my husband, Kyle. He is truly a gift and is the leader of our family. I cannot wait to see him be a father one day, but until then, we will serve the Lord with all we have, together. Thank you Kyle for all your love and support! Love you!

Letter to a loved one

I cannot tell you how many times I have been asked, *what is the best thing to say to someone who is struggling with infertility?* Maybe you are reading this book hoping to find that answer because you love and support someone who is feeling defeated in this battle. It is a hard and true question.

As humans, we crave knowledge and answers. Yet some situations, like infertility, offer inconsistent answers, hard answers, and sometimes lonely answers. As humans, when we see someone hurt, it is really easy to get uncomfortable and not say anything, ask questions that come out wrong, or give advice in an area in which we have no business doing so. The best thing to do is be bold and ask questions about the person's journey.

Talking about infertility draws people out of their isolation, even for just a moment. Be aware, you could get tears, hard stories, details that are too much information, or you may get vague answers, but your interest and care reaches them in the hard lonely place.

My encouragement for you when you talk with someone you know is struggling with infertility is to ask specific questions about his or her journey. Try not to respond with advice, thoughts, or feelings, but just listen to what they are saying.

Ask those you talk to what the Lord is teaching them in this journey and if there any passages of scripture have been encouraging or guiding. Ask them if they feel the Lord is trying to tell them something or lead them towards specific decisions. And then—this is the hardest part—do not give advice or tell them things that have worked for other people.

Each person is different and his or her answer and guidance from the Lord is different. I cannot tell you how many conversations I have had where I say what I have been learning and the person responds with other methods that have worked for other people. Then I typically feel deflated and have felt like the person who gave me their ear did not actually listen to a word I said and just wanted to give me advice. And then later, when I am alone, I start to think about this advice over the instruction that the Lord gave me. Anything that is different than the Lord's instructions is a false sense of hope.

Ending a conversation is always hard, but do not expect yourself to know what to say. Offer to pray for the person, or say you will check in with them in some time, or leave them with a scripture that has been on your heart. I do believe God uses people as guidance through tough times, but it should align with where the scriptures are leading. That is why it is important to listen and ask questions about their next steps and what God is teaching them or where He is leading them.

People expect you to always have a plan and the knowledge of what to do, but what happens when your "plan A" is not working? As the body of Christ, we need to love on, support, and encourage each other not to have self-confidence or solutions, but to seek God. God is truth and has all the answers. He has your plan and will reveal steps and solutions in His timing, not ours.

To the Secret Club Member - *There is no perfect conversation, no perfect answer, no perfect question. It is important to have grace for people who are trying to communicate with us and help us. No one is perfect, and in a tense or sensitive conversation, it is hard to find the right time, let alone the right words. Try to tune your ears to the heart* *of what people are saying and try to seek opportunities to share Christ's love regardless of harsh words or insensitive comments.*

Encouraging Playlist

Throughout my journey, God used worship and music to encourage and guide me. In the darkest moments, the right song would play and allow me to cry out to the Lord in sorrow and in praise. I wanted to share a list of songs that impacted me along my journey.

Scars - I AM THEY
Nobody - Casting Crowns (feat. Matthew West)
Thy Will - Hillary Scott & The Scott Family
Surrounded (Fight My Battles) - Michael W. Smith
Broken Vessels (Amazing Grace) - Hillsong Worship
It is Well - Bethel Music & Kristene DiMarco
Transfiguration - Hillsong Worship
Strong God - Meredith Andrews
Living Hope - Phil Wickham
Over All I know - Vertical Worship
Awake My Soul (A Thousand Tongues) - Matt Maher
Yet Not I But Christ In Me - Selah
Held - Natalie Grant
Find Me in the River - Cast of I Still Believe
Keep Me in The Moment - Jeremy Camp
Songs In The Night - Matt Redman
Behold The Lamb - Passion (feat. Kristian Stanfill)
King of My Heart - John Mark McMillan
Even If - Mercy Me

Endnotes/Bibliography

1 - Catalyst Healthcare Marketing. "13 Infertility Stats You Should Know." *Fertility Answers,* 11 Jan. 2017, www.fertilityanswers.com/13-stats-know-infertility/.

2 - Tommy's Pregnancy Hub. "Tommy's - How Common Is Miscarriage?" *Tommy's Pregnancy Hub,* 2015, www.tommys.org/pregnancy-information/im-pregnant/early-pregnancy/how-common-miscarriag e.

3 - NW, 1615 L. St, et al. "Childlessness up among All Women; down among Women with Advanced Degrees." *Pew Research Center's Social & Demographic Trends Project,* 25 June 2010, www.pewresearch.org/social-trends/2010/06/25/childlessness-up-among-all-women-down-amon g-women-with-advanced-degrees/.

4 - Penn Medicine. "Secondary Infertility - Penn Medicine." *Www.pennmedicine.org,* 2021, www.pennmedicine.org/for-patients-and-visitors/find-a-program-or-service/penn-fertility-care/secondary-infertility. Accessed 2 June 2021.

5 - Southwestern Eye Center. "The Science behind Why We Cry." *Southwestern Eye Center,* 26 Apr. 2019, www.sweye.com/blog/optical-care/the-science-behind-why-we-cry/. Accessed 2 June 2021.

6 - Doucleff, Michaeleen. "NPR Choice Page." *Npr.org,* 2019, www.npr.org/sections/healthshots/2013/12/30/258313116/mapping-emotions-on-the-body-love- makes-us-warm-all-over.

7 - Warren, Kay. *Choose Joy*. Grand Rapids, Michigan, Revell, A Division Of Baker Publishing Group, 2012.

Waiting In Hope. "Medical Terminology." *Waiting in Hope,* 2020, www.waitinginhopeinfertility.com/terminology. Accessed 2 June 2021.

Armstrong, Stephen. "The Letter of James | Verse by Verse Ministry International." *Versebyverseministry.org*, 2010, versebyverseministry.org/bible-studies/the-book-of-james. Accessed 10 Aug. 2021.

The author's biblical interpretations and conclusions presented in this document rely on original teaching by Verse By Verse Ministry International (VBVMI) used by permission.

The author's views do not necessarily represent the views of VBVMI, its Directors or staff. Original VBVMI teaching may be found at http://www.vbvmi.org."

About the Author

Bianna Lindenmeyer is a high school science teacher in Kansas City, Missouri. She is married to Kyle Lindenmeyer and together they run a photography company. Over the years they have been greatly impacted by their struggles with infertility and pregnancy loss. Connect with Brianna or share your story at:

www.TheSecretClubBook.com

Made in the USA
Monee, IL
05 November 2021

81276373R00104